# QUEST FOR RENEWAL

# QUEST FOR RENEWAL

## Personal Revival in the Old Testament

**Walter C. Kaiser, Jr.**

MOODY PRESS

CHICAGO

Library of Congress Cataloging-in-Publication Data

Kaiser, Walter C.
    Quest for renewal.

    Includes index.
    1. Church renewal—Biblical teaching.  2. Bible.
O.T.—Criticism, interpretation, etc.  I. Title.
BS1199.C45K35      1986           269           86-5374
ISBN 0-8024-7050-5 (pbk.)

3 4 5 6 7 Printing/BC/Year 90 89

*Printed in the United States of America*

To the Reverend Robert W. Smith
and his wife, Violet,

for ten years of faithful pastoral service during my teens and for
a memorable candidating sermon, which began to stir my
interest in the Old Testament: Hosea 10:12, "Break up your fallow
ground, for it is time to seek the Lord, that He may come and
rain salvation upon you."

# Contents

# Foreword

The psalmist prayed, "Wilt thou not revive us again: that thy people may rejoice in thee?" (Psalm 85:6, KJV). It was the cry of one who wanted God's people to come alive to His grace and power. That is what revival is all about—the restoration of something to its true nature and purpose. Inasmuch as all of us were made to glorify God, revival simply fulfills His desire that we might know Him in the fullness of His Spirit and declare His praise to the ends of the earth.

Few will question the need for such an awakening today. For many good people, even within the church, life has lost its meaning. There is no sparkle in the eye, no spring in the step. As the religious community flounders in mediocrity, the world plunges deeper into sin. Moral standards in public and private are debased. Everything is unsettled. Lawlessness abounds. All the while a cloud of nuclear destruction gathers overhead.

The day of reckoning is sure to come. Degeneration has its limits. The crises must be resolved, or inevitably there will be judgment. That point of no return may be nearer than any of us imagine.

But there is hope. In other days when catastrophe threatened, men and women turned to the Lord and found in Him deliverance and strength. It can happen again, if the people of God will meet the conditions for revival.

This book can help us focus the issue and make the appropriate response. With penetrating insight, it shows what God can do when His sovereign will is acknowledged and obeyed. By uncovering spiritual principles inherent in great awakenings of the Bible, the author leads us to know how to prepare the way for revival today.

Dr. Walter Kaiser, distinguished dean of Trinity Evangelical Divinity School and professor of Old Testament and Semitic languages, has earned the right to be heard. A renowned Hebrew scholar, his teaching and writing is revered in centers of learning wherever the Scriptures are seriously studied. He speaks to the heart as well as to the mind. The transparent sincerity of his own witness shines through it all. One can not go through these accounts of revival without being moved to higher aspirations and nobler actions.

Years ago, after the funeral of General William Booth of the Salvation Army, the sexton of the church found a lone Methodist preacher on his knees at the altar. Still thinking of the tremendous influence of the life of the godly Booth, the preacher was overheard to say, "O Lord, do it again! Lord, do it again!"

That is how I felt as I read these pages. I trust that you, too, will find yourself praying that revival will happen again, that persons of faith will come forth who will believe God for the impossible, and that their numbers will increase until a new and mighty demonstration of holy love sweeps over the land.

"Lord, wilt thou not revive us again: that thy people may rejoice in thee?"

Robert E. Coleman,
author of
*The Master Plan of Evangelism*

# Introduction

When in the course of human events there lies such a heavy sense of injustice and despair over the prolification of evil and the failure of any forces for good or righteousness to carry the sentiment of the day, there remains only one answer: revival. This has been the experience of men and women throughout history, as the biblical record testifies.

If I (and a host of other observers of Western culture) am not wrong, the time is again ripe for that outcry to heaven from mortals who sense that things have got out of hand, that the forces of sin, evil, and destruction are beyond our ability to contain. For example, in just one decade this country has almost tripled Hitler's record for destruction of human life with our sinful flaunting of regard for the unborn. Hitler slaughtered 6 million Jews, and we have put to death more than 15 million babies. The question of the hour is this: if God judged Germany for her evil, then why has He not judged the United States?

Not that this is our only sin; it is merely the most sensational offense. Our sins are growing out of all manageable proportions, including child abuse, pornography, homosexuality, failure to require capital punishment, and widespread corruption in the halls of justice and government.

However, when evil and wickedness seem to grow like weeds on the landscape, God has often graciously sent His people, as the first signal of revival fires, a deep yearning for relief that knows no other language than the cry for deliverance. (Five times in the history of the Judges things got so bad that finally misery found a voice to cry out to God.) It is only then that the human predicament presents God's first opportunity to be heard clearly and fairly. In my judgment, we in the United States and Canada have arrived at just such a time, and therefore it is time for revival in North America.

What then is revival? Probably this is one of the church's most abused terms. Some see it as a synonym for mass evangelism or a special week of meetings in the local church aimed at winning the lost to Christ. Others regard the term with suspicion and automatically associate it with bizarre happenings in church meetings held under heavy orgies of emotion. Tales of emotional extravagances abound, such as barking like dogs, the "jerks," and theatrical feats of showmanship on the part of both the subjects of revival and the revivalists themselves.

But neither of these understandings can claim biblical support for what is distinctive or normative about revivals. Indeed, one of the most amazing facts about the whole subject is that in spite of a rather extensive literature of several thousand volumes on the topic, I have been able to find only five volumes (two of which are quite slender) that treat the subject of revivals in the Bible. These volumes in the order of their publication are:

> Baker, Ernest. *The Revivals of the Bible*. Capetown, South Africa: Miller, 1906. Pages 1-181.
>
> Smith, Wilbur M. *The Glorious Revival Under King Hezekiah*. Grand Rapids: Zondervan, 1927. Rev. ed. 1954. Pages 1-54.
>
> Newell, Philip R. *Revival on God's Terms*. Chicago: Moody, 1959. Pages 1-48.
>
> Autrey, C. E. *Revivals of the Old Testament*. Grand Rapids: Zondervan, 1960. Pages 13-160.
>
> Olford, Stephen F. *Heart-Cry for Revival: Expository Sermons on Revival*. Westwood, N. J.: Revell, 1962. Pages 7-128.

As long ago as 1937, Wilbur M. Smith observed that

> the Christian Church still awaits a scholarly examination of [the] sixteen Biblical revivals, set in their historical perspective, with a very careful study of the various ways in which the Spirit of God moved upon a nation, or a city; in other words, a work comparable to that done in relation to post-Biblical revivals by James Burns in his epochal *Revivals: Their Laws and Leaders*, issued in London in 1909.[1]

1. Wilbur M. Smith, *The Glorious Revival Under King Hezekiah* (Grand Rapids: Zondervan, 1937), pp. vi-vii.

Although the present work cannot claim to be everything that Smith was looking for, certainly there is much to be learned from examining ten of the great Old Testament revivals. Inasmuch as revival remains the prerogative and special work of God, it would appear that the first requisite for any significant planning, praying, or writing in this area would be the study of revivals in the Bible.

What then is the Bible's definition of revival? Almost everyone will agree that the greatest text on the subject is 2 Chronicles 7:14, "If my people, who are called by my name, will humble themselves, and pray, and seek my face, and turn from their wicked ways, then will I hear from heaven, and I will forgive their sin, and I will heal their land." The text does not use the term *revive* or *revival*, as does Psalm 85:6: "Will you not revive us again, that your people may rejoice in you?" However, there can be little doubt that 2 Chronicles 7:14 supplies most of the components of a definition. It identifies the *subjects* of revival (not just Israel, but all who are owned by God and have God's name on them), the four *conditions* for revival (the same ones featured in the four key revivals that are reported by 2 Chronicles, providing its structure, as I will argue), and the three *results* that form the special work that makes revivals unique, distinctive among all the works of the Lord.

Moreover, the context of 2 Chronicles 7:14 identifies the *circumstances* where revival might apply. King Solomon had just completed his magnificent prayer of dedication for the recently completed Temple. The prayer included the request that God would forgive the nation's sin whenever it had forced Him to introduce drought, famine, and pestilence (2 Chron. 6:26-31). It was in reply to this request that the Lord responded in 7:12-16, in words that provide both the basis and formula for all true revivals.

No doubt a significant number of God's people will object that 2 Chronicles 7:14 has no reference to them because it was addressed to Israel; it is strictly not their mail. But though the desire for a consistent hermeneutic, which underlies this objection, is admirable, the conclusion is wide of the mark on several counts. First of all, the phrase "If my people" is immediately glossed, or explained, by the little epexegetical, or appositional, clause "who are called by my name," a clause so distinctive to both Testaments that its meaning could never be confused or mistaken. What God or man named, he owned and protected, whether that included cities (2 Sam. 12:28; Jer. 25:29; Dan. 9:18-19), the Temple (1 Kings 8:43; Jer. 7:10, 11, 14, 30; 32:34; 34:15), or men and women (Isa. 4:1; Jer. 14:9; 15:16). Thus when Israel walked by faith, Moses promised that "all peoples of the earth shall see that you are called by the name of the Lord" (Deut. 28:10). In the same way, James noted how God had "visited the Gentiles to take out of them a people for His name" (Acts 15:14). Most convincing of all is the appearance of the phrase in Joel 2:32 "all who call on the name of the Lord will be saved." Those who did not believe were "like those who [were] not called by my name" (Isa. 63:19). The fact that Peter used this expression on the day of Pentecost to inaugurate the age of the Spirit, the New Covenant, and the church is not altogether accidental. Therefore, although this promise was originally given to Israel, it is also most assuredly intended for us.

Another reason for applying this promise to present day believers is that it involves the same hermeneutical principle as the one used in applying the New Covenant to the church. The New Covenant in its original setting was clearly addressed to the house of Israel and the house of Judah (Jer. 31:31), apparently setting aside all claims of the church to the promise. But we are ministers of the New Covenant (2 Cor. 3:6), and we do drink the blood of the New Covenant in the Lord's Supper (Matt. 26:28; 1 Cor. 11:25). It is true, of course, that the climactic fulfillment of the New Covenant will not come until "the Deliverer comes to Zion and He banishes ungodliness from Jacob" in that day of the restoration of Israel to her Lord and her land (Rom. 11:25-27). Thus without (incorrectly, in my judgment) simply equating the nation Israel with the church, it is possible to see that what appeared to be an exclusive word to Israel included the believers of the New Testament era. The "people of God" are one, even though we can distinguish several aspects, such as believing Israel and believers in the church.

Finally, the assurance given in Romans 15:4 and 1 Corinthians 10:11 should keep us from insulating the contemporary Christian from 2 Chronicles 7:14. Paul teaches, "Whatever was written in earlier days was written for *our* instruction, so that . . . from the Scriptures *we* might have hope," and, "All these things happened as types of *us*, and they are written for *our* admonition, upon whom the ends of the ages has come" (italics added).

The centrality of 2 Chronicles 7:14 for the study of revivals in the Bible can be witnessed by the fact that it provides the outline for 2 Chronicles and sets the agenda for the material selected from the lives of five key Davidic kings of Judah. Each of the four *conditions* for revival is taken up separately as the single most important term for the reigns and lives of these five Judean monarchs. The resulting pattern forms an *inclusio*, with the first and last king sharing the same term. It may be plotted as follows:

| Imperative | 2 Chronicles | King |
|---|---|---|
| "Humble yourselves" | 11-12 | Rehoboam |
| "Seek my face" | 14-16 | Asa |
| "Pray" | 17-20 | Jehoshaphat |
| "Turn from your wicked way" | 29-32 | Hezekiah |
| "Humble yourselves" | 34-35 | Josiah |

Fifteen of the thirty-six chapters in the book, or almost one-half of the material, are given over to the reigns and revivals of these five kings, for they honored God during their reigns by leading their people in revival. It is not an extravagant claim, then, to see the theme of revival as one of the central organizing motifs of 2 Chronicles. In fact, another recent commentator on the book has also observed:

> It is quite extraordinary that none of the commentators has seen the vital significance of [2 Chron. 7:14] for the Chronicler's theology. . . . Four avenues of repentance are mentioned which will lead God to forgive and restore, and these are taken up at various points in the remainder of the narrative and illustrated. . . . That this is deliberate is shown by the fact that wherever these terms occur in the earlier narrative they are often quite neutral theologically and do not mark similar miraculous turning-points.[2]

By now it is clear that a revival can only be defined in terms of something happening to the believer. For Stephen Olford revival is "the sovereign act of God, in which He restores His own backsliding people to repentance, faith and obedience."[3] Likewise, Charles Finney wrote, "It presupposes that the Church is sunk down in a backslidden state, and revival consists in the return of the Church from her backslidings and in the conversion of sinners."[4] Even though Finney in-

2. H. G. M. Williamson, *1 and 2 Chronicles*, The New Century Bible (Grand Rapids: Eerdmans, 1982), p. 225.
3. Stephen Olford, *Heart-Cry for Revival: Expository Sermons on Revival* (Westwood, N. J.: Revell, 1962), p. 33.
4. Charles G. Finney, *Revivals of Religion* (Westwood, N. J.: Revell, n.d.), p. 7.

cluded the conversion of sinners as part of his definition, it is clear
from his book that he viewed this as an effect and not as part of the
initial work of revival. "The fact is," warned Finney, "*Christians* are
more to blame for not being revived than *sinners* are for not being
converted."[5] C. E. Autrey agreed: "Revival is a reanimating of those
who already possess life. . . . It revives spiritual life which is in a state
of declension."[6] In short, in the words of the Old Testament prophet
Hosea, revival consists of "breaking up fallow ground," which once
had been tilled and was mellow and suitable for growing an abundant
harvest but now is hardened and overgrown with weeds and all sorts of
spontaneous vegetation—none of which pleases or is useful to the
farmer (Hos. 10:12). Perhaps the most succinct definition of revival
has come from J. Edwin Orr, who has written extensively on the subject in our generation. With an eye to Acts 3:19, he affirmed the best
definition of revival is the phrase "times of refreshing from the presence of the Lord."

The assumption is that revival is needed to remedy deficiencies that
would not be present if real Christianity were being practiced and readily observed by a watching world. Whenever such authenticity is
scarce, it becomes necessary to plead, "O Lord, revive your work in the
midst of the years" (Hab. 3:2). Accordingly, revival presupposes a serious decline in the church's appetite for spiritual things and in her
championing the cause of morality and justice in human affairs.

Furthermore, revival presupposes that believers either do not know
the standards set forth in Scripture or do not care to press them as the
basis for deciding what is true, just, righteous, beautiful, and pleasing
to God. And when Christ's followers have ceased to function as salt and
light (Matt. 5:13-16), society and the church are left without any principle or purpose when judged by the norms given in the Word of God
and consequently without any check on ungodliness. Wickedness
grows like weeds, and no voices are raised in protest or warning about
the certainty and awesomeness of the frightening judgment of God
that is to come. Thus, the consistent lack of obedience to the will of
God among Christians is the problem underlying the need for revival.

Even more embarrassing, however, are the telltale signs of deca-
dence within the church itself. This is amply illustrated in our own
day. It is bad enough that the world exhibits sins that only a few years

5. Ibid., p. 20.
6. C. E. Autrey, *Revivals of the Old Testament* (Grand Rapids: Zondervan, 1960), p. 13.

ago the most godless man would have turned away from in revulsion; now the same list of sins is shared by the church of the living God. Surely revival is needed when believers fall into such vices and scandalous sins as incest, abortion, divorce, homosexuality, cheating of employers and the government, and immorality. Revival is also needed when worldliness so captures our hearts that we are as entrapped by our insatiable desires for leisure time, extended vacations (away from the house of God), and every kind of entertainment as the ancient Israelites were by the idolatry of the Canaanites. Of course there is a legitimate theology of leisure and culture in Scripture (e.g., the joy of life as traced in Ecclesiastes; see my small commentary on that book), but when any form of leisure or entertainment competes for the believer's time and loyalties, equaling or exceeding the time and joy that he gives and receives from spiritual things, then he has crossed the line and entered headlong into idolatry.

Another signal that something is wrong in the church comes when a spirit of controversy arises over minor issues or even in the way in which major issues are handled. The presence of a party spirit, jealousies, dissensions, and whisperings about fellow believers, other denominations, churches, institutions, mission agencies, and the like indicates a desperate need for revival. The Christian life cannot flourish apart from an environment of love and brotherly concern no matter how grievous the error or the difference among believers may be. This, too, has a current application.

But if deviations like these are not only known among our churches and Christian institutions but also widely reported and tolerated, we should not be surprised by our relative ineffectiveness or the fact that the world does not take us very seriously. Is it any wonder that the wicked continue to triumph in the marketplace and in government in opposition to the spread of the gospel? Our sins have had the net effect of reducing to a new level of impotency the efforts of pastors, evangelists, and missionaries to spread the gospel. Can water rise higher than its source? Can the Christianity reproduced on the fields of the earth fail to reflect the level of spiritual experience or the fervency of supportive prayer found in the sending church in North America? When the wicked become bold, insolent, reckless, and arrogant in establishing new lows for morality and godlessness, there righteousness has suffered a staggering blow because of the laxity of professing Christians. Such a time will be filled with terrorists, murderers, extortionists, crooks, thieves, whoremongers, and haters of God.

There is, however, an all-too-convenient explanation for latter-day spiritual decline that has been used frequently, but mistakenly, by sincere evangelicals: the imminency of the Lord's return. But this truth of Scripture is too wonderful a teaching to be strapped with the burden that these "weasel-Christians" would like to foist on it. Things indeed will grow worse among the wicked as we approach the time of the end. But this fact was never meant to be used as an excuse for our own lack of purity or as a means for trying to outguess the Lord as to when this day would come. Faithfulness is always the first prerequisite of the watching, waiting, and praying believer looking for the Lord's return. Surely we can derive no satisfaction from the fact that the world is going "to the dogs," as if this would speed things along. In fact, the only way we can hasten the day of the coming of Christ according to 2 Peter 3:12 is by living holy and godly lives.

Therefore, today's believers must begin by following God's program for revival as set forth in 2 Chronicles 7:14, or our land will lie fallow and overgrown. On the other hand, if we are willing to repent of our sin, however tenuously at first, then the floodgates of heaven will open, and both we and our culture will be the surprised recipients of the blessing of God.

The cost is significant, however. Every area of neglect and omission must be explored by each individual: the failure to love God with all of one's heart and soul or to show concern for the eternal damnation of the lost outside of Christ; the neglect of earnest prayer, of the diligent study of Scripture, and of the health of our own souls or the souls of our brethren in the household of faith; the omission of duties to family and society. In addition, there is the need to probe our scarred consciences for sins of commission. The list is too long to attempt here, but surely it begins with sins of the heart, such as envy, pride, ill will, jealousies, and hatreds, before it goes on to involve deeds of the flesh, such as lying, stealing, immorality, cheating, and all of their ilk.

How can the preaching of the gospel at home or abroad have any major effect, or how can Christians act as salt and light in society, when our hearts are frozen and in a fallow state? All our efforts for spiritual service will be handicapped and seriously curtailed in their real impact when judged by the standards of the resurrection power of Christ if we do not soon experience a genuine Holy Spirit-attended revival.

What then are the features of revival as described in the Scriptures and especially in the ten great Old Testament revivals on which this book focuses? Wilbur Smith lists nine characteristics of the great revivals in the Old Testament.[7]

First, most revivals were preceded by a time of deep spiritual decline and despair. For example, there was the Egyptian bondage, which led to the golden calf debacle, or the time prior to the revival under King Hezekiah, which involved the revolting practice of offering children as burnt offerings on the altar of Molech. No different was the situation in Elijah's time, with the maddening spectacle of a whole nation gathered on Mount Carmel, unable to decide whether to worship Baal or Yahweh. All were times of deep spiritual decline, and they match our own in many ways.

Second, each of these revivals began in the heart of one of God's servants, who then became the instrument in God's hands to stir up the sleeping consciences of God's people. The list of revival leaders includes the patriarch Jacob; prophets like Moses, Samuel, Elijah, Haggai, Zechariah; kings like Rehoboam, Asa, Jehoshaphat, Hezekiah, Josiah; and leaders like Nehemiah and Zerubbabel. The truth of God, which these leaders brought to the people, was the great motivating force for revival, not the mere charisma of their own persons or the dynamic of some managerial ability otherwise unknown or untapped until that time.

This leads nicely into the third characteristic. Every revival in the Old Testament rested solidly on a new and powerful proclamation of the Word of God. The most obvious evidence of this characteristic can be seen in the revival under Josiah, when the book of the law was found and read with great response in the presence of the king. In the revival that took place under Jehoshaphat, the Levites "taught throughout Judah, taking with them the book of the law of the Lord" (2 Chron. 17:9). No less central was the Word of God in the revival under Ezra and Nehemiah, for Ezra read from it from daybreak until noon (Neh. 8:3) for seven days (Neh. 8:18), "making it clear and giving the meaning" (Neh. 8:8). But even in those instances where the revival was not immediately preceded by a proclamation or reading of the Word of God, such as with Jacob or Elijah on Mt. Carmel, the power and ministry of that mighty word is not very far out of the picture. All lasting revivals have their genesis in the restoration of the Word of God to its rightful place of prominence. As Wilbur Smith warned:

7. Smith (rev. ed., 1954), pp. 7-8.

A revival which does not rest solidly upon the Word of God will ultimately either fade out, because there is no fountain of divine truth continually refreshing it, or it will run into dangerous and sensational emotionalism, which, after it has passed, will make those who have been the subjects of such an experience dry and indifferent to the things of God, at times more easily accessible than ever to the inroads of Satan himself. There is something about the Word of God that men recognize as divine: when it is preached men know that they are hearing the Word of God, and nothing less will ever arouse a nation sunk in selfishness, self-satisfaction, and godlessness.[8]

The fourth characteristic is that each revival was marked by a return to the genuine worship of Yahweh. Whether it was Jacob smashing the idols of his family, Elijah exposing the impotency of Baal, or Haggai calling for authenticity in the worship and service of the Lord, they all presented the same case. Wholehearted, genuine worship of the living God became the chief delight and one of foremost desires of each person who was truly restored to spiritual vitality. Hence the great corrective needed for most current complaints about worship lies primarily not in the area of form, setting, or even substance but in the area of a new reviving work of the incomparably great God.

Closely attached to this is the fifth sign of revival: a destruction of every idol that blocked the rightful acknowledgment of Yahweh as the only true and living God. This is true of every revival except the last two, which occurred after the Exile, when no idols were left in Judah. It is easy, of course, to dismiss this characteristic in the modern era with a sense of relief: "At least that is one sin we do not possess or need to worry about!" But we are involved in idolatry, even if we do not possess icons or plaster and metallic images, whenever we allow any concept, program, committee, goal, commitment, person, or pleasure to take a place equal to or greater than that which rightfully should be occupied by the Lord alone. God will not share His glory or honor with another, whether that be a sports team, the television, a job, family, or some overwhelming aspiration.

In the sixth place, there was a deep sense of sin and an overpowering desire to separate themselves from it and from all its sponsoring causes. Such divinely induced anxiety and agonizing conviction of sin needs no prompting or psychological maneuvering. The work is uniquely that of the Holy Spirit. The failures of the past, even those

8. Ibid., p. 25.

that have been forgotten, suddenly become so real and so painfully present that no amount of comfort or personal rationalization will assuage the terrible pressure of individual guilt and heartbreak. Accordingly, so spontaneous and thorough should be the conviction and simultaneous hatred of sin that there will be no need to plead with men and women to make any decisions.

In every revival in the Old Testament there was likewise a return to the offering of blood sacrifices. Given such a heavy sense of sin, there must be as great a remedy, and that can only be met by the one and only sufficient sacrifice of the Paschal Lamb of God. Every sacrifice in the Old Testament pointed forward to the final sacrifice that Christ would offer. Thus in Hezekiah's time there was mention of the sin offering (2 Chron. 29:21-25) and the first reference to atonement since Israel came into the land (2 Chron. 29:24). Only on this basis could the people be revived; all other schemes were bogus deals.

The eighth feature that is plainly set forth in the Old Testament revivals was the experience of a new sense of unbounded joy and exuberant gladness. Nowhere is this seen more clearly than in that postexilic scene with Nehemiah and Ezra. Instead of permitting the people to continually weep and grieve over their sins, Nehemiah and Ezra counseled them to stop mourning, for that day of revival was sacred to the Lord. It should be a day for celebrating, feasting, and sending gifts, for "the joy of the Lord is your strength" (Neh. 8:9-10).

The ninth and final characteristic is that each revival was followed by a time of great productivity and prosperity. This is not the health, wealth, happiness, and success message that some are offering today. Rather it is the observation that the fortunes of the soil are intimately tied up with men and women and their spiritual success or failure. We find the rationale and explanation for this feature of revivals in the biblical record as early as the Garden of Eden. When Adam sinned the ground was cursed on his account. And so it will remain until all creation is redeemed at the future coming of the Lord (Rom. 8:20-22). But if the final redemption cannot presently be offered because creation is still subjected to vanity, there can be substantial healing in the realm of nature.

This observable measure of healing for the fields and crops of the fields is always associated with the repentance of humanity and the revival of the spiritual fortunes of believers. Thus Haggai asked whether anyone had noticed that when the spiritual temperature of the community declined, so did the productivity of their fields, the enjoyment of their food and drink, and the purchasing power of their earnings (Hag. 1:5-6). Similarly, in response to the preaching of Joel's call for repentance, Yahweh answered not only with a promise of the future outpouring of the Holy Spirit (Joel 2:28-32) but also with immediate relief from the locust plague and the drought (Joel 2:19-27). The fields, Joel explained, would groan under the heavy load of the bumper crop of grain and grapes. The pastures would become green, the trees would bear their fruit in abundance, and the autumn and spring rains would come as before. The barns and storage bins would overflow because the yield would be so unexpectedly high.

We should not be surprised, therefore, to find that 2 Chronicles 7:14 promises that God will heal our land if we turn to Him in order to be revived. Must we always fail to see that the deliverance offered in Scripture is not isolated from the material world? It is not enough to view the effect of revival as only on a person's soul. Revival affects the whole of life, including agriculture, the economy, international relations, peace, and the security of a people (even in its large urban areas). To be sure, revival is no panacea or magical cure-all. To see it as such would be to reject the reality of the presence of sin in the created order until Messiah's return. But neither should we hesitate to speak of the substantial restoration that is available now. It is to our shame that we have not utilized our spiritual power more openly and effectively; but then, how can we if we are currently in need of being revived? Before we can either experience these blessings or be the means of blessing to a watching world, revival must come.

Before turning to examine ten Old Testament revivals in detail, there is a final question that needs to be considered. Some may still be asking why it is necessary to study the revivals of the Bible. There are at least five good reasons for exposing ourselves to an in-depth study of biblical revivals—yes, even the revivals of the Old Testament.

The first reason is motivational: a study of the biblical revivals ought to create a desire in the believer for revival today. Seeing God graciously grant His power and presence to those who so obviously had earned anything but God's mercy and grace is a strong source of encouragement to us. In this sense, the study of revival is contagious. Every legitimate inducement, especially from the Word of God, is a further encouragement for us to sense our own condition before God.

The second reason is more methodological. It answers the question, How should we go about the quest for revival? What methods will God use? For example, in some of the revivals of the past, God used a national crisis (as at Mizpah under Samuel) or a three-year drought and an outdoor meeting on Mt. Carmel (under Elijah) as the occasion for times of refreshing from the Lord. Moreover, when individuals or the believing community could not be reached by the faithful preaching or teaching of the Word of God, God made that Word scarce. Eventually, those who had become deaf to the message of the Word were forced to listen to another, harsher, word from God: the harsh realities of a culture without the purifying presence and gracious provision of the hand of God. Then it was, and still is, that man's extremities become God's opportunities. If we have not observed this yet from experience, then the Word of God is still available to teach us.

A study of Old Testament revivals will acquaint us, in the third place, with the types of people that God uses in revivals. In themselves they were nothing spectacular. They possessed the same desires, fears, and successes that many of us experience. Therefore we should be careful about making plaster saints out of them. But we do develop a great respect for the God these men adored and trusted implicitly. We learn how they went to the school of prayer, as Elijah did for three years, before they were used of God in one great day of ministry to turn a whole nation to God. We learn that what they were externally they first were in their hearts, for "as a man thinks within himself, so is he" (Prov. 23:7).

We are instructed, fourthly, on how we should prepare for revival. The stress in 2 Chronicles 7:14 on the four conditions for revival are amply illustrated, taught, and urged in every one of the ten great Old Testament revivals. It must be acknowledged that much ink has been spilled over the question of the proper source and means for expecting a revival. However, most of this debate could have been settled long ago by a full and patient listening to Scripture. This battle over whether revival is solely and always the work of God, or whether it also recognizes certain means that are requisite to promote a revival, has sorely tried the church in the past and will no doubt be used by the enemy of our souls and of revivals on every future occasion. Few will deny that God is sovereign in this whole work of revival, but many will doubt whether men and women have any necessary part. Yet, most, if not all, will agree that man is not just a robot, without any fault or responsibility in this affair. And surely confession and repentance, even though they are aided by the special work of God, are nonetheless also the responsibility of individuals.

The debate in this area reminds me very much of the debate that has been raging over the doctrine of sanctification. As a student I sat through many sermons by speakers who asked the audience the rhetorical question, Do you know what is wrong with Christians? Why it is that we are so far behind our beliefs in practicing a vital, sanctified life? The first time I heard this question I was all ears, for I had no idea what the desired response was. It turned out to be this: it is because we are not willing to Let Go and Let God. The proof for this statement was found in such texts as Ephesians 2:9-10, "For we are His workmanship," and Philippians 2:13, "For it is God that is at work in you both to will and to do His good pleasure."

Well, that settled that question. At least it settled it until the next day when another chapel speaker arrived and rhetorically asked the identical question. Had it not been a dignified and most conservative setting, I might have blurted out yesterday's answer, but fortunately for my reputation and the reserved decorum of the setting, I was spared what would have been certain embarrassment and great theological discomfort. As it turned out, the answer had changed 180 degrees overnight. Now the problem was not the "emptiness of busyness" as a substitute for the sovereign working of God; no, the problem now was that too many Christians were lazily sitting around expecting God to do everything when the Scripture said, "We are created unto good works" (Eph. 2:10), and that we should "work out our salvation with fear and trembling" (Phil. 2:12).

It took a number of months and years of this kind of switch-hitting before I began to realize something (typical case of a slow learner). Both sides were appealing to almost the same contexts or verses. However, each was quoting only that portion of the text that held high the point in the argument they wished to make. My conclusion suddenly was staring me in the face: Scripture taught both positions, and one without the other was in danger of becoming lopsided.

Thus I conclude that there can be no revival without the Lord's initiating it and carrying it out. But I also conclude that no one can hide behind the doctrine of God as the explanation for why we have not had a revival in our day or the reason that the last great revival in America occurred in 1905-06. There are requisite factors for revival, such as repentance, prayer, the preaching of the Word of God, humbling ourselves under the mighty hand of God, and earnestly seeking His face. The study of the ten great revivals of the Old Testament should handily demonstrate both the balance and the dual nature of this truth without clumsily involving us in a despicable works-salvation or even in any whisper of a suggestion that we or anyone else has merited, earned, attracted, or otherwise been responsible for the favor of God.

The fifth and final reason for studying revival involves the area of preparation. Once we know how the Lord has acted in the past, we should be better prepared to accept the special working of God when it arrives. It will also warn us that no two revivals are alike, for the Lord God uniquely suits each divine visitation to the needs of the hour. Every one of our preconceptions and built-in limitations concerning what God can or cannot do or what He is likely or not likely to do in exact detail must be jettisoned if we are to learn anything from the distinctiveness of each of these Old Testament revivals.[9]

Let us now turn to each of these ten teaching passages where the Word demonstrates the truth of 2 Chronicles 7:14 and the power of a revived people of God.

9. I am indebted for this general list of five reasons for studying revivals (though without attributing the substance and general development of the discussion) to Autrey, pp. 18-20.

# 1

## It Is Time to Get Rid of Our Idols:

### REVIVAL UNDER JACOB
### Genesis 35:1-15

**W**ere it not for the shocking events of life, some of us would never consider our need for revival to be very serious at all. But often, just when we have settled into the routine of our ways and thought that we were no worse off than the average believer, the Lord mercifully shocks us from the staleness of our relationship with Him. How much easier it would have been to have listened to the Word of God in the first place. But God's love is so intense and so deeply desirous of our good that when we become deaf to His Word or fail to respond to it, He mercifully knows how to get our attention through the events of life. Of course He would rather have us respond to His Word without this special prompting. But when all else fails and after a long period of patience, then God speaks to us as individuals and as a nation through the problems and tragedies of life.

This is not to say that God is the author of evil. He is holy, pure, and without any sin whatsoever. He is no more the author of evil today than when Satan appeared before Him in the book of Job to request permission to bring tragedy into Job's life. Of course the purpose of those calamities was different from the ones presently being considered. In Job's case the purpose was to answer the challenge that people serve God only because He blesses them. However, in either case it is clear that evil is only permitted by God. He is the author of the author of evil in that He created Satan before he sinned. Therefore, although God can and does allow evil or tragedy to come into our lives, He is not its author.

One of the reasons God would allow such a horrible thing to happen to us is to alarm us of the seriousness of the plight of our spiritual health and progress. We do not live by bread alone but by every word that proceeds from the mouth of God. It was in just such a circumstance that the patriarch Jacob found himself in Genesis 35. The whole problem started over his daughter, Dinah, one of his children by his wife Leah.

Jacob had just moved back into the land of Canaan from Paddan Aram (Gen. 33:18) when Shechem, the son of Hamor, ruler of that area, saw Dinah, took her, and raped her (Gen. 34:2). This tragedy set off a string of events that would permanently alter the lives of all who were touched by them. Nevertheless, God was still in control, allowing His will to be worked out in spite of the violence and reprehensible evil involved.

Hamor came to Jacob to negotiate marriage, settle the bride-price, and establish friendly relations only to learn that there was trouble. Dinah's brothers in particular were outraged: "Such a thing should not be done" (Gen. 34:7). Hamor offered favorable terms, involving the reciprocal offer of intermarriage between their families, but he had no understanding of the impossibilities this presented for a people who were not to be unequally yoked to unbelievers. But then, what real difference was there between these unbelieving Shechemites and Jacob's family? In practice their lives seemed to be alike.

Jacob had promised God some thirty years earlier, when he was fleeing the wrath of his deceived brother, Esau, that if God would be with him, watch over him, and return him safely to Canaan, then Yahweh would be his God, and he would serve Him. But like so many of us in these so-called foxhole experiences, Jacob had forgotten his vow. Yet God had returned him safely to his land, and had blessed him, and had caused his life to overflow with the bounty of God's goodness (Gen. 28:20-22). How, we ask in amazement, could Jacob have been so ungrateful? Surely he had nothing when he cried out for help. And was thirty years not enough time to remember the vow made to God, or even to remember Yahweh Himself? Perhaps Jacob considered himself a self-made man; after all, had it not been by his own hard work, wits, and sheer will-power and drive that he had become what he was? This argument ("I earned it by myself") sounds curiously similar to the attitude of the average middle class or newly rich American today. But now there was family trouble, and that was different.

To make matters worse, there was more trouble, for Jacob's self-made sons decided to take things into their own hands and reap vengeance on the heads of Hamor's clan. First there was deceit: the sons pretended that all would be well if the men of Hamor would be circumcised; then Dinah could be given in marriage (34:13-16). Is it not true that once evil is let loose, sometimes there is no stopping it except through a genuine change in the lives of all who were affected? But in this situation Jacob still did not see the hand of God or the necessity for calling his sons or these heathen to repentance. In fact, he had even forgotten his own vow to God.

The situation deteriorated further. The men of Hamor's city yielded to the demand to be circumcised, totally unaware of what evil lay lurking in the hearts of Jacob's sons. On the third day after this operation, while they were still in pain, every male in the Canaanite city, including Hamor and his son Shechem, was murdered by Jacob's sons (34:25-26). None of this had the approval or consent of Yahweh.

Only then did it begin to dawn on Jacob how serious a situation he had worked himself into. For when the looting and the stealing of all the livestock and goods was over, Jacob rebuked his two sons Simeon and Levi, who had reaped this havoc on the offenders: "You have made me a stench to . . . the people living in this land. We are few in number, and if they join forces against me and attack me, I and my household will be destroyed" (34:30, NIV). Their only defense was to retort, "Should our sister have been treated like a prostitute?" (34:31, NIV).

It took an atrocity like this to push Jacob to finally take the action he should have taken a long time ago; it was time he and his family took this word to heart: "Get rid of your foreign gods" (35:2). I believe this text is the focal point of Genesis 35, providing the basis for a threefold challenge. Thus I have used it in the title of the present chapter. Chapter 35 gives three *reasons* Jacob, his sons, and *we* ought to get rid of our idols. They are:

1. Only cleansed men and women can meet God (vv. 1-4).
2. Only God can protect us when we are in danger (vv. 5-8).
3. Only God can change our personalities and bless us (vv. 9-15).

Consider each of these reasons one at a time as we enter into an exposition of the passage.

### Only Cleansed Men and Women Can Meet God (35:1-4)

In the midst of Jacob's bitter reflections and agonizing perplexities, the Lord urged Jacob to move his family approximately thirty miles south of Shechem to Bethel. This was the very spot where Jacob had sought God in a moment of deep despair some thirty years before. Here he had experienced the heavenly vision of a ladder, and here he had made his vow. In other words, God ordered him back to ground zero. It is too bad that it had taken a crisis to drive Jacob to this point, but it was better for him to have the crisis and to respond than to miss the blessing of God.

How important it is to fulfill the vows we have made. Jacob's deliberate delay had cost him the grief experienced with his daughter, Dinah. The same lesson would later be repeated with Moses, who sinfully delayed in circumcising his son, due apparently to a family argument over the rite with his Midianite wife, Zipporah (Ex. 4:24-26).

What a stern warning this is to us as well. So frequently we have no idea that there is a subtle and pernicious drift away from divine things in our lives or in our families until it is almost too late. Then events shock us to our spiritual senses and force us to take drastic and speedy spiritual measures for the saving of ourselves and our households.

It is interesting to note, as George Bush comments, that God did not order Jacob to "build an altar to me as you promised and disappointingly have not done lo these thirty years."[1] Instead, Genesis 35:1 simply says, "Go up to Bethel and settle there, and build an altar there to God, who appeared to you when you were fleeing from your brother Esau." The remonstrance is ever so gentle a reminder, not casting in Jacob's teeth all the trouble he had brought on himself because of his stubbornness. There are so many evidences like this of grace in the Old Testament that we can never forget that the nature of God has always been the same, and it ever will be.

The time had come to get back to God quickly. The savagery and cruelty of his sons had convinced Jacob of that. Even though there was a cost for Jacob's hesitancy to make God Lord in his life as he had promised, there still was time to put away the root of these problems.

1. George Bush, *Notes of Genesis*, 2 vols. (1860; reprint, Minneapolis: James and Klock, 1976), 2:200.

Surely there is a lesson here for us to learn.

There can be little doubt that the source of decay in this family could be traced back to the presence of foreign gods in their midst. Sometimes it seems so easy just to let some things be, but these little sins can become like foxes that burrow away in our lives until their appetite knows no limit and they have devoured us.

In the Introduction a strong connecting link was observed between idolatry in another day and the contemporary challenges that come in the form of every rival of God in heart, mind, and life. Therein lies the real genius and penchant for idolatry, both ancient and modern. Nothing can have first place along with the Lord: not my job, my hobby, my goals, my organizations, my leisure time, my recreation, my marriage, my family, or even my church. If such are placed first or even share first place with my commitment to the Lord, then I have slipped into idolatry. In this case, Baal, Anat, Asherah, Molech, and all other rival gods have captured my silly heart.

Jacob's word, and hence God's word to us, is straightforward: "Get rid of them" (v. 2). Furthermore, He urges us to "purify ourselves" and to "put off [our old] clothes [and put on new]."

We may wonder whether Jacob himself partook in any of the practices associated with these icons or if he was aware up to this point of his children's practice. Had he been unwilling to risk the resentment of those who were dear to him by ordering the removal of these gods? Indeed, where had the gods come from? By way of answer, Rachel, Jacob's favorite wife, spirited away the gods, or teraphim, of her father, Laban (Gen. 31:19). Scholars believe that whoever possessed them was also owner of all the family property; thus they functioned, if we may judge from archaeological references in tablets from that approximate epoch, as wills to inherit the property. But did they also tempt their owners to worship as well? Or did the entrance of this evil come from the Mesopotamian servants, who had become syncretistic in their faith, professing to worship Yahweh while holding on to remnants of their old pagan ways? One other possibility occurs to us. Could these have been the gods stolen from the sacking and looting of Shechem? (The Targum *Jonathan* refers to them as "the gods which you received from the house of the idols of Shechem.") The correct answer is that we simply do not know. But the result was the same regardless of their origins. Get rid of them; that is God's command to all His people.

In addition to this command, the Lord challenges us to personal holiness. The command to "purify [our]selves" was again expanded by the Targum *Jonathan* as "Cleanse yourselves from the pollutions of the slain to whom you have come nigh." But this hardly meets the total demands of the text; Jacob's family was filled with more impurities than the mere contact with corpses. Surely the changing of their clothes merely symbolizes the putting off of the old and the putting on of that which was new.

Holiness of life is never satisfied solely with one aspect of man to the exclusion of all others. This theology can be illustrated with Moses' experience at the burning bush. When he was told to take off his sandals, he must have felt authentic and comfortable in those shoes. Why should he have to take them off? But Yahweh patiently explained that because He was present and because the ground Moses was standing on was holy, he needed to obey.

The lesson is clear: holiness is *wholeness*. In fact, the English root for both words is one and the same. Both the secular and sacred English words come from the same root. Therefore, it will do no good to prepare to meet God only in our hearts or, conversely, with mere outward vestments, excluding real inward preparation. For the believer, holiness is not an optional spiritual luxury, nor is it an unessential feature, if we expect to see revival in our time.

After adequate and holistic preparation had been made, the house of Jacob could approach the altar of God (v. 3). And this was the place of forgiveness for ruptured relationships. On no other grounds or bases could full restoration to the favor, fellowship, and reviving energy of the living God be possible.

Suddenly Jacob recalled his old promise and the fact that God had "answered [him] in the day of his distress and had been with [him] wherever he had gone" (v. 3). If we ask why this command to build the altar had not come sooner, the response will be the same as the reason God lets us go on so long with matters degenerating to such a terrible state of affairs that only a crisis is left to awaken us from our lethargy. Harold Stigers accurately commented:

> So it is that God leaves His people to their ways so that they and others, seeing such results, may understand why believers should *not* live for themselves and earthly things to the exclusion of the will of God. Yet when they repent, as did Jacob, God is gracious to forgive. But the scars remain; the scars for Jacob were the lives led by his sons.[2]

2. Harold G. Stigers, *A Commentary on Genesis* (Grand Rapids: Zondervan, 1976), p. 262.

Just as 2 Chronicles 7:14 would later promise, so here also God promised that He would hear from heaven and answer. Moreover the expression "in the day of distress" in connection with prayer must have been on the mind of the psalmist when he wrote in Psalm 20:1, "May the Lord answer you when you are in distress; may the name of the God of Jacob protect you. May he send you help from the sanctuary" (NIV). And that had indeed been the experience of Jacob, for Yahweh had been with him, He had watched over him wherever he had gone, He had brought him back to his own land, and He had not abandoned him even when Jacob did not appear to have merited such gracious treatment (Gen. 28:15).

When God promises to answer, He intends to say more than that He will merely acknowledge the petition with either an affirmative or a negative. Rather it means that He will effectually work on the petitioner's behalf. That is what happened when He answered Elijah by fire (1 Kings 18:24), and so it will be for our earnest petitions as well.

The surrender and dedication of Jacob's family was completed by the surrendering of their gods and earrings (which apparently served as charms, amulets, or talismans). Thus all superstitious reverences were abandoned and buried under the oak at Shechem, which, incidentally, may be the same oak near which Joshua later set up a stone of witness (Josh. 24:25-26).

But we are surprised to see such ready cooperation after so many years of neglect. Why? George Bush answered when he observed, "The incident teaches us that where our spirit is right, we have great access to the hearts of others. Duties [which are normally] difficult in prospect are rendered easy and successful the moment we have . . . faith to carry them into execution."[3]

## ONLY GOD CAN PROTECT US WHEN WE ARE IN DANGER (35:5-8)

When God places His repentant people under His protection, they are safer than they would be under some military DEW defense line or if they were protected by a whole arsenal of weapons all in dense pack. His people no longer need to be overly concerned about what their enemies might be planning. Neither do they need to keep up the pretense that good-for-nothing idols can save them. (This would amount to little more than using a rabbit's foot.)

3. Bush, p. 201.

After Jacob's household had purged itself of all idolatry and returned to a full acknowledgment of the only true and living God, an astounding dread fell on their would-be detractors because of a divinely induced terror sent from God (v. 5). Once again the grace of God exceeded all the steps of faith taken by these men towards God. The Lord placed such high restraints on those who normally were vindictive that no one pursued Jacob and his family. And not only was this restraint felt by those who were directly affected, but the neighboring towns, whose populations were by far much larger than Jacob's small entourage, also decided against any pursuit of Jacob. If only we as North Americans could learn (indeed, if all the nations of the world could only learn) that our best defense does not lie primarily in our material hardware or the state of our military preparedness but in a renewed visitation of the Spirit of God in response to our decision to rid ourselves of all our idols.

Moving to Bethel signified more than moving to a place of safety; it was also a place of reconciliation at the altar of God. This altar, built by Jacob, was the fifth altar built by the patriarchs, for Abraham had built altars near Bethel (Gen. 12:8) and Hebron (Gen. 13:8), Isaac had built one in Beersheba (Gen. 26:25), and Jacob had also built one in Shechem (Gen. 33:20). Previously Bethel had been named Luz, meaning "almond tree," but that name, which Jacob had given to it thirty years earlier, had not yet taken hold. From now on it would be known as Bethel, meaning "the house of God," because it was here that Jacob had met with God in the past, and here it was that sacrifices would be offered on the altar of God (v. 7).

In renaming Luz *El Bethel*, Jacob unmistakably connected God's name with this site. In Hebrew, the word *El*, the shortened form of *Elohim*, or God, is distinctly separated by the Hebrew disjunctive, a separating accent mark used in the post-Christian system devised by the Hebrew scribes known as the Masoretes. The name *El*, then, is not part of the title, for in that case the place would be called (in translation) by the clumsy name "God, house of God." Some scholars think, though it is difficult to say for sure, that *El* or *Elohim* by itself signifies that God is the strong one, the miracle-working God who had been protecting and blessing Jacob all during those twenty years in the land of Paddan Aram. But what we can say for certain is that Jacob, if he ever was involved in the polytheism of his sons, is certainly done with it now. Verse 7 places the article in front of the proper name for God (a fairly uncommon phenomenon), thus making it clear that He is the one true living God.[4]

Two wonderful hallmarks of revival now appear in the text: the revelation of God and the place of sacrifice. Where would we be without a word from God and a means of reconciliation and atonement? It was the Lord Himself who took the initiative in communicating with man (even as He did when Jacob was thrown on his own resources and felt himself a stranger from the promises of God). And it was the Lord who invited Jacob to set up an altar. This place of death would be a picture of life to all who would claim the promise of God until He would come and personally do what no animal or human rite ever could do or promise to do. Only the word of acceptance by God combined with the authorized picture of what God would one day accomplish was the guarantee that stood behind this place of slaughter, as the word *altar* literally signified. The altar and the Word of God—these were God's means of reviving His people. And in that security, all danger was negligible, for greater was the Lord they now served than all the threats, weapons, machinations, and armies of men.

## Only God Can Change Our Personalities and Bless Us (35:9-15)

When God graciously grants a revival to come into our lives, there are a number of changes. Not only do we experience freedom from the fear of our enemies, as Jacob witnessed in the preceding section, but there is a reorientation of our personalities. Thus it happened that Jacob received a new name.

Biblical names are more than just the vocable by which individuals are addressed. In ancient Israel they were also used to indicate the nature, character, and personality of a person. So it was that up to this point Jacob carried a name meaning "supplanter," or "he who grasps the heel" (Gen. 25:26). For that is how Jacob came into this world: he came out of the womb clutching the heel of his brother Esau who had preceded him. And that is the way Jacob made his own way through life (at least that is what he thought). But it was God who constantly pursued him, even when Jacob acted as if he were the only one responsible for what he had and what he had become.

On two occasions God met Jacob and so overpowered him by His love that he would forever remain changed. In Jacob's early years,

4. H. C. Leupold, *Exposition of Genesis,* 2 vols. (Grand Rapids: Baker, 1953), 2:919.

when God first appeared to him in the dream of the ladder to heaven prior to his leaving Canaan, the Lord was already calling him into a new and fuller relationship with Himself (Gen. 28:13). But at Peniel Jacob spent a long night in wrestling with the Angel of the Lord, who is identified in Hosea 12:3 as none other than God Himself: "In the womb he grasped his brother's heel; as a man he had power [or, struggled] with God." At Peniel Jacob's name was changed to *Israel,* which means "he struggles with God." The Lord explained, "Your name will no longer be Jacob, but Israel, because you have struggled with God and with men and have overcome" (Gen. 32:28, NIV). Jacob named that place Peniel because, as he said, "I saw God face to face" (Gen. 32:30, NIV).

The second occasion was after the Dinah incident in Genesis 35. Once again God said, "'Your name is Jacob, but you will no longer be called Jacob; your name will be Israel.' So he named him Israel" (Gen. 35:10, NIV). Apparently the trauma of the first episode—Jacob was on his way home from Paddan Aram after many years and filled with fears about what his brother Esau, whom he had cheated, might do to him——had not served its full purpose. Jacob was still Jacob in heart and spirit. Yet tragedy had accomplished what a lifetime of wrestling with God could not. Not even a whole night of confrontation with God face to face had stirred his slumbering soul. After the Shechemite massacre, however, Jacob's sleepy soul was aroused. Henceforth he would become a prevailer with God in prayer (Gen. 35:9). The long divine pursuit of Jacob had climaxed.

How much will it take before some people respond? How patient must God be? How long must He wait before we catch on and are revived and changed thoroughly? One thing is certain. When we put away our idols and purify ourselves under the mighty hand of God, the Lord changes our names, that is, our personalities, our characters, our natures, and our dispositions.

But there is more. When we put away our idols, the blessings of God, which lay dormant and only in word form, come to us in full measure. Revival does not necessarily mean that these blessings are totally new. Often they are those we have already experienced. But now they come with a freshness, force, and power not known during the days of our lackluster, dull, yawning, and equivocating walk with God.

In 35:11 the Lord announces Himself as *El Shaddai,* a name used rather infrequently in the Old Testament (forty-eight times), mostly by the patriarchs and Job, who probably lived in the same era. The oldest interpretation of the name goes back to pre-Christian times when the Greek translation of the Old Testament, the Septuagint, rendered it as *pantokrator*, "all-powerful." Likewise the Latin Vulgate said *omnipotens*. The rabbis analyzed the name as being a compound composed of the relative *she*, "who," and the word *day*, "enough"; hence, "the one who is [self]sufficient" (Babylonian Talmud, *Hagigah* 12a). Recent scholarship has not progressed much beyond these pre-Christian and early Christian interpretations. The ending *-ay* certainly makes it an adjectival suffix; hence, "[something] of the . . ," but we are no further in identifying the actual root. Therefore it is best to understand it as a testimony to the effectiveness, sufficiency, and power of God.[5] God appeared as *El Shaddai* to the patriarchs seven times: to Abraham (Gen. 17:1), to Isaac (Gen. 28:3), and to Jacob (Gen. 35:11; 43:14; 48:3). The context for every one of these instances was the promise-plan of God, which in itself should tell us something about the name: He is the all-powerful one and the God of all-sufficiency.

This promise-plan of God stretches from one end of the Bible to the other. At its heart is the gospel: "In your seed all the nations of the earth will be blessed" (Gen. 12:3; Gal. 3:8). But it takes its inception from the very ordinances of creation itself. The ancient promise that God would make His own fruitful and that He would multiply them is repeated in 35:11.

The statement exceeded anything personal and individual and went on to include a nation that would come from Jacob; in fact, a whole community of nations. More accurately, they were to be a *qahal*, a "congregation" of nations. Was this the tip of the iceberg, a harbinger of the whole future missionary movement that was to come—the fact that God was here and now empowering and commissioning Israel to be His witnesses to the nations? In my opinion, yes.

The centerpiece of this promise doctrine was the fact that a king would come from the kings that were to flow out of the loins of Abraham and Jacob. From that patriarchal line, and eventually from the Judean kings, the Messiah would be heralded. The man of promise would come from Jacob's own body (35:11)—wonder of wonders and mystery of mysteries.

The sphere in which one aspect of this promise-doctrine would un-

---

5. Victor P. Hamilton, "Shaddai," in *Theological Wordbook of the Old Testament*, 2 vols., ed. R. Laird Harris, Gleason L. Archer, Jr., and Bruce K. Waltke (Chicago: Moody, 1980), 2:907.

fold would be the Promised Land. Accordingly, God would not only bring His blessing and salvation to the inner lives of these revived men and women, He would also demonstrate that He was the Lord of all history and the Lord of all real estate by assigning a tithe of the lands of the earth to be the instruments of His good news to the nations. This promise is very much part and parcel of His over all promise-plan. It was just as perpetual and eternal as were the so-called spiritual parts. It would serve as a perpetual sign to the nations that the Lord had the legal claim to all territories of the world. Thus He claimed a small portion in perpetuity as a symbol of this right (35:12).

After revealing all these blessings, which were in the main a repetition of the ancient words given to Abraham and Isaac, especially when He had appeared to them as *El Shaddai,* God "went up from above him" (literal rendering of 35:13). This implies a visible manifestation by God to Jacob just as he had experienced years ago at Bethel and more recently at Peniel. It is also similar to the experience of Abraham in Genesis 17:22, where God likewise "went up from him."

In commemoration of this outstanding episode, Jacob memorialized it by setting up a "standing stone" (35:14), for it is always good to remember those times when we have met God in a new and wonderful way. He also went on to consecrate the spot where God had performed a reviving work of grace in his life by anointing the standing stone with oil and by pouring out a libation (see Ex. 29:40; 30:9; Deut. 32:38). And once again Jacob named the spot Bethel (v. 15) as he had in Genesis 28:19 after his vision of the ladder to heaven.

Thus revival came to the house of Jacob because he was willing to get rid of the idols in his life. There is our challenge as well. Are we tied to the past, with its toys and ambitions that steal our hearts from loving God with everything in us? Do we have the courage to hear God's word in our day? Will we act with all due speed in the church to cleanse our lives of all this filthiness? Or will our families, churches, institutions, and nations continue to suffer because of the moral *minority's* failure to come to grips with the most pressing spiritual need of the hour?

Our appeal to all believers everywhere is this: let us turn from our competing loyalties to the living God, renounce all forms of wickedness, especially those involving idolatry, and act quickly before the love of God is forced to drive us to even greater calamities than we are currently facing in our lives and our society. Then we shall find the same great blessing that Jacob found for himself and his house.

# 2

# It Is Time to Confess Our Sin:

## REVIVAL UNDER MOSES
## Exodus 32:1—34:7

**N**othing so separates us from the Lord as sin. It is this thief that robs us of the benefits of our standing in the Savior. It is this blockage that renders us impotent before the present system of evil and wickedness. Alas, due to the corrosive and corrupting power of sin, the believer with all his mighty potential, the salt and light for which this world hungers, is unable to function as intended. These two tragedies, the tragedy of our separation from God and the tragedy of our uselessness, are reasons enough to call for an immediate confession of sin and a prayer for God to begin His reviving work in every one of us.

Nowhere in Scripture is this need evidenced more dramatically than in the situation found in Exodus 32:1—34:7. There are few places in the Bible where such a wonderful expression of God's compassion and full forgiveness can be found simultaneously. Moses had been called to the top of Mt. Sinai to receive the law of God. But when his absence seemed to stretch out longer than they thought it should, the people panicked. All sorts of wild scenarios began to form in their minds, where the peace of God should have resided. They imagined that Moses had been struck by lightning or killed by some other violent or natural means. Therefore, they began to take matters into their own hands.

Their first thought was to replace God with other "gods who would go before [them]" (Ex. 32:1). No one remembered that Jacob and his sons had been through this routine not too many years before. Instead, they pummeled poor Aaron with questions and urged him to cast a new, visible god that would replace the one worshiped by their absent leader, Moses. The sheer treachery of the request is enough to make us, at this safe distance in time and space, cry out in outrage on behalf of the offended Lord. But none the less treacherous are our stupid sins. There should and must be the same outcry of grief over them. For, like Israel's sin, they have severely offended a holy God, separated us from His favor, and rendered us impotent in the great cause of justice and righteousness here on earth.

Unfortunately, Aaron does not seem to have protested too much. Further, it would appear that he did not even attempt to dissuade them. His advice came quickly: "Take off the gold earrings . . . and bring them to me" (Ex. 32:2). These he used to cast an idol in the shape of a calf. And this was the same Aaron, Moses' brother, who was consecrated as high priest to Yahweh. He fashioned the monster with a tool and then, strangely, announced a festival to the Lord (v. 5). Once again we are back into the heavy drag of syncretism, that system that attempts to serve God and mammon. But how is this possible? How can we serve two masters? Will we not, as Jesus taught, love the one and hate the other?

There is another sin present here. The rabble-rousers showed disregard for their leadership when they whined, "As for this fellow Moses . . . we do not know what has become of him" (32:1). Surely their tone showed anything but appreciation and regard; it was disdainful and cynical. How quickly the erring heart forgets all the mercies and gifts of God given to His people through delegated leaders. This, then, becomes a further sign that we are ripe candidates for revival. When we easily reject the leadership that God bestows, it may signal that our hearts, more than the abilities of the leaders given to us, are in serious need of repair. Thus, we trade symptoms for causes and fail to face ourselves, all the while trying to relocate the blame and facilely assign it to some remote category, such as the personalities and abilities of our leaders.

On completion of his monstrous act of blasphemy, Aaron had the nerve to declare, "These are your gods, O Israel, who brought you up out of Egypt" (v. 4). He also added an altar for offerings to this bull-calf (an all too easily identifiable icon left over from their days of witnessing the idolatry in Egypt; cf. Apis, the bull-god of Egypt).

By now everything was out of hand. Out came the drinks, and away went the garments, and Israel was totally out of control. Sin always begets more sin in its wake, and it spreads like the rot. When the English text says they "rose up to play" (32:6, RSV), it means the people began to indulge in sexual prostitution. (The same verb is used to describe Isaac "fondling" his wife in the marital act; cf. Gen. 26:8.) Therefore, the compounding of sin was a major problem. Israel risked losing all the promises of God by openly flaunting their rejection of God. What will the Lord do to them for this outrage?

The answer is not long in coming. So serious was their offense that God threatened to destroy the whole nation, excepting Moses. To him He would grant all the promises that had been pledged to the patriarchs (32:18). At the very least He would withdraw His presence from the nation and refuse to be with them any longer (33:3).

This sets up the marvelous teaching of the grace of God in forgiveness. No where else does such stark contrast appear between the utter failure of human sinfulness and the absolutely limitless power of Yahweh to cleanse. The only limitation on the application of this free grace and forgiveness is to be found in Israel's (and our) stubbornness. Yet how senseless and irresponsible is refusal, given the high degree of vulnerability in sinful situations. Accordingly, we should be warned against the unnecessary *risks* involved in not confessing our sin. According to Exodus 32:1—34:7 and the life of Israel, there are at least four:

1. The risk of facing the anger and wrath of God for our sin (32:7-14)
2. The risk of facing the loss of atonement for our sin (32:30-35)
3. The risk of facing the loss of the presence of God for our sin (33:1-17)
4. The risk of facing the loss of the goodness of God for our sin (33:18—34:7)

As 2 Chronicles 7:14 reminds us, repentance, turning from our wicked way, is an extremely important component of meeting the prerequisites for a genuine revival. Sin leads us to a defeated position. If we continue in it without major changes involving a heartfelt confession of sin, we open ourselves up to untold mischief. The risks are almost incalculable. The Lord's plea (cf. the urgency of this text) is that we might profit from the warning of Israel's example, flee as quickly as possible to the merciful side of our Lord, and claim His restoring grace. May the rehearsal of each of these risks do more than merely move us cognitively. May they stir us to mourn over our sin.

## We Risk Facing the Anger and Wrath of God for Our Sin (32:7-14)

There is no sense in trying to hide our sin or to pretend either that it is not there or that it is not as bad as it first seemed. Sin will not just disappear by itself. Even if we bury it deep in our subconsciousness, it will still need to be dealt with. The reason is given in the text: God knows, hears, and sees all the words, thoughts, and deeds of humanity. For, though Moses was yet on Mt. Sinai, the Lord informed him that things had got out of hand on the plain below (vv. 7-8). Yahweh quoted verbatim to Moses what Aaron and the Israelites were saying. He also saw the calf and was aware of their bowing down to it and worshiping it. Nothing is hidden from His eyes. That is the point we will need to come to realize in this whole matter of sin. It is not what we can get away with when those who might censor us would know; it is what God sees, hears, and records that is at the heart of the problem of sin. It is amazing that the people thought that neither Moses, whom they judged to be dead, nor God, their Lord and provider of the covenant, saw or cared about their partying and gross sin. But while men and women sported on the plain, their conduct was being viewed from above.

God's indignation is clear from His very first word to Moses, *"your* people . . . whom *you* brought up out of Egypt" (v. 7). It is also clear that He regarded sin as lawlessness, for Israel had turned away from what He had commanded (v. 8). No wonder He referred to them as "stiff-necked" (v. 9), a metaphor referring to bullocks who refuse to have their necks brought under a yoke.

In a striking figure of speech, God is depicted as if He were beyond all remedial discussion due to this great offense against His law and His person. The Lord spoke in such a way as to test Moses. "Leave me alone," He said, "that my anger may burn against them and I may destroy them. Then I will make of you a great nation" (v. 10). What *seemed* to be a command not to petition God in prayer on behalf of His sinful people was in reality a high testimony to the effectiveness and power of prayer. For if God could see that prayer would be so potent in persuading His offended holiness to exercise mercy, then we as believers had better flee more quickly and more frequently to this retreat. But there is more; God could also see that the man He had prepared these eighty years would do exactly what He in His sovereignty had taught him to do: he would besiege Him in prayer as a mediator on behalf of these sinners. The situation was as George Bush assessed it:

> The words . . . which *seemed* to forbid, were *really* intended to encourage Moses in his suit. They are not indeed a positive command to him to pray in behalf of Israel, but they indicated what it was that would stay the divine hand from punishing; and were equivalent to saying, "if you intercede for them, my hands are tied, and I cannot execute the deserved vengeance."[1]

The counteroffer, to make a great nation out of Moses instead of continuing on with Israel, might have been very tempting to some people. This offer assaulted Moses in the area where most men are vulnerable: his pride. But Moses was totally disinterested. The long years of learning through the experiences of life now paid off. God's man had grown in grace. Moses' previous hot temper and superquick responses to raw injustice and wrong were now tempered by the very patience God had exhibited on his own behalf time and again.

The man whom God had prepared to be a leader and mediator began to earnestly entreat his Lord. His initial questions in verses 11 and 12 are not expostulations but examples of places in Scripture where the interrogative can be used for the optative mode. Moses made a threefold plea: (1) do not let the Egyptians rejoice over the ruin of those they hate; (2) do not forget the covenant You made with the patriarchs; and (3) do not destroy so quickly what You have employed so much power to preserve and bring this far (vv. 11-13). The real goal of his prayer was, as the goal of all true prayer should be, the glory of God.

Meanwhile the people who were the objects of this prayer were casting off all restraint and running wild (32:25). It is a curious fact that the same verb used twice in this verse is also used in Proverbs 29:18, which says, "Where there is no vision [i.e., a word of revelation from God or a proclamation of that word to His people], the people *break loose* [i.e., they cast off all restraint, become unmanageable, and they

---

1. George Bush, *Notes on Exodus* (1852; reprint, Minneapolis: James and Klock, 1976), p. 215, emphasis his.

apostatize]." Rather than urging individuals and churches to have a five-year or ten-year plan (which, incidentally, is a good idea), the verse in Proverbs warns us about the lawless state of affairs that will result when other programs and priorities are substituted for the Word of God.

## WE RISK FACING THE LOSS OF ATONEMENT FOR OUR SIN (32:30-35)

When he saw the sin of Israel, Moses' initial reaction was violent; in fact, in a rage that is not altogether excusable, he heaved to the ground the tablets written by the finger of God. Then, in a call for a division of the house, he summoned all who were on the Lord's side to come over to him (32:26). Only the Levites responded, surprisingly enough—those who belonged to Aaron's tribe. (There is irony for you.) Next, Moses commanded these volunteers to strap on their swords and to go through the camp executing all the ringleaders of the rebellion. Three thousand were slain.

On the next day Moses lectured the people about the enormity of their sin (Ex. 32:30). "Great sin" may be a technical name for this type of immorality, for the phrase is found in a few other ancient Near Eastern records and in the attempted seduction of Joseph by Potiphar's wife (Gen. 39:9). One should not, however, automatically rank this sin higher than other sins on a scale of wickedness. It would appear from verse 30 that not all the guilty died with the three thousand of the preceding day. That is why I referred to the latter group as ringleaders. Those who were exempted from death on that occasion were not permitted to draw the false conclusion that their guilt was less serious, for Moses charged them with having sinned a "great sin."

"Perhaps I can make atonement" must have been the sweetest sounding words the heavy consciences of these wild sinners had heard in the previous twenty-four hours. The point of the expression is not that Moses was in doubt whether there was an atonement but rather whether he was the instrument. Again Bush is most helpful:

> He thought he might perhaps be *an instrument of reconciliation*; for in no other sense could *atonement* be properly predicated. . . . He was not without hope, nor yet was he destitute of fear; accordingly his words were calculated to preserve the people in a due medium between desponding dread and presumptuous confidence.[2]

2. Ibid., p. 224, emphasis his.

This same mode of address is used elsewhere in Scripture to both encourage sinners and protect them from being overly presumptuous about the grace and forgiveness of God. Amos 5:15 says, "It may be that the Lord . . . will be gracious"; Jonah 1:6 has a similar word, "If so be that God will think of us"; and Acts 8:22 likewise comments, "If perhaps the thought of your heart may be forgiven." God's forgiveness is free and always available, but we must not trifle with it, cheapen it, or use it in such a way that we become casual about the seriousness of our offense against the command and person of the living God.

God had prepared Moses for this role of being an intercessor and mediator. Both ministries were anticipations of our own deep need of someone who would come from heaven, pray for us, and be our mediator. Already in patriarchal times, Job had cried out for a mediator, a defense attorney who would be his advocate (Job 9:33). Now Moses would fill in this gap on behalf of the Lord as he began to pray in one of the few interjections in the Bible: "Oh, what a great sin these people have committed!" (32:31).

The plea of the mediator was that God would forgive. So emotionally worked up was Moses and so deeply affected was he by their sin that verse 32 is an incomplete sentence. He leaves the ellipsis after the alternative, "and if not. . ." This heightens the impassioned and pathetic tone of the prayer. It is as if we, the readers, are being allowed to be in the same place where the sobbing prayer of God's servant is being poured out before God. (See 1 Sam. 12:14-15 for a similar conditional sentence.)

"Nothing is so efficacious," comments Bush, "in obtaining mercy as deep humiliation before God."[3] But we are shocked to hear Moses offer to be "blot[ted] out of the book you have written" (v. 32). The offer sounds very much like the apostle Paul's wish that he could be accursed if only it would lead to the salvation of his brethren, the Jews (Rom. 9:3).

What is the book Moses referred to? Psalm 69:28 mentions a "book of the living," and Philippians 4:3 a "book of life." Later on, Isaiah 4:3 will refer "to be[ing] written with the living." So what did the expression mean at the time Moses spoke? Did he wish to die early rather than witness the destruction of his people? Or is he offering to yield up his place as one of the redeemed in order to ransom his people, that is, exchange his life so that the people might be released from the guilt of their sin?

3. Ibid., p. 224.

Surely no human life, no matter how valuable or godly, can be sufficient to atone for anyone's sin, much less for the sin of a whole nation.
The Egyptians had the practice of recording the names of those who
hoped to be associated with the pagan deity in the afterlife. Moses,
however, must have been aware of the existence of such a record in
the divine counsels of God. The expression, then, was a gesture on
Moses' part of his deep sorrow for his people and of his recognition
that they had no basis on which to plead for the mercy or favor of God.
Unless God was moved to exercise His own mercy because of the prayer of His mediator, there would be no hope.

The offer of volunteering his name in exchange for the deliverance
of all these people was unnecessary. The theology of individual responsibility for one's own sin was clearly set forth: "Whoever has sinned
against me I will blot out of my book" (v. 33). This is the same teaching that would be stated so frequently in that great chapter of Ezekiel
18, "The soul that sins, it shall die." Everyone is responsible for his or
her own sin.

The sin of the people resulted in a major shift. In the past the Lord
had led Israel, and Moses had only been there as His servant (Ex. 3:8;
12:42, 51; 13:17; 20:20). But now Moses and an angel (not the Angel of
the Lord, that is, Christ Himself, in whom resided the very essence
and being, or "name," of God; 23:20-21) must lead them. So rather
than the Lord and His servant, a servant and the Lord's messenger
become the guides and leaders of Israel. That was a significant loss.

In addition, a "day" of judgment when sin would be punished was
promised. The phrase, literally,"in the day when I visit" (v. 34), is
probably the first reference to the much discussed "day of the Lord"
mentioned so frequently by the prophets. This was not just any old
day; it was to be *the* day of God's visiting, one day that stood out
supreme over all other days. Later revelation would make it clear that
this day could be a time of national judgment in the immediate future.
However, it also signaled an even greater time of trial, not only for
Israel but for all the nations that had turned their backs on the only
true God as well. Accordingly, for the calf-worshiping sinners of the
Exodus, the near aspects of that day commenced when the Lord struck
Israel with a plague, much as He had already visited the Egyptians
with a plague prior to the Exodus (Ex. 7:25; 8:2; 12:23, 29).

How risky it is to try to wait God out with an unrepentant heart. We
need His atonement, for how else will we be able to be at one with
Him?

## WE RISK FACING THE LOSS OF THE PRESENCE OF GOD
### FOR OUR SIN (33:1-17)

In its most risky feature of all, sin separates us from the presence and goodness of God. What person or community can long exist without His helpful and restraining influence? Yet, the presence of God cannot coexist where there is sin, especially gross sin.

Exodus 33:1 is probably more accurately rendered as a pluperfect, "The Lord *had* said." It is thus a continuation of 32:34, where the Lord was still speaking to Moses. The general effect of the message from God was still the same, for Israel had shown as yet no special signs of repentance. Therefore the signs and reality of the divine presence were withdrawn immediately. Sin does indeed cut us off from God. In fact, under such sinful conditions, it would have been even more dangerous for the divine presence to remain. This would have increased Israel's responsibility and their exposure to punishment. That is why those of us in the Western nations, who have been so privileged in experiencing so much of the presence and power of God, are all the more vulnerable. We will be dealt with much more speedily and harshly than the other nations, who have not been so privileged.

But thanks be to God, Israel's long delayed cry for help finally came (33:4). Why is it that we poor sinners are so reluctant to call for help when we know we are drowning? Is it that we are too proud to admit that our basic need is to humble ourselves under the mighty hand of God? The people began to mourn and to strip off (the same verb was used in Ex. 3:22 of Israel's "despoiling" the Egyptians; also 12:36) their ornaments. This latter action signified that they had begun to humble themselves under God's hand. Thus the text repeats this significant and most blessed development in verse 6: they had humbled themselves.

Verse 5 may give the appearance that God was in some doubt or perplexity as to what He should do. Again, however, it is only by way of accommodation to our impoverished understanding that He speaks in this way. Truly God is never at a loss as to what He should say or do. His perplexity, if there be such, concerns not whether He should show mercy but how to display it so as to act consistently with His honor. Once Israel humbled themselves in genuine repentance (and not just in attrition, that is, sorrow over the fact that they were caught) for their sin, there was no longer any apprehension over how God might act towards His erring children. Therefore the language of doubt is deliberately used to imply that there was a plan and special design to the mercy of God once mortals repented.

The identification of the tent mentioned in verses 7-11 poses some problems for the interpreter. Possibly it was a temporary tent specially constructed to hold the ark. Or it may have been one that Moses set up outside the camp as sort of a second home and the only place where the presence of God would meet him (the presence of sin in the camp handicapped that function there). One thing is certain: this could not have been the Tabernacle itself, for that had not yet been built (Ex. 35-39). Regardless of how we answer this question, the important point was that God had withdrawn His presence, and He had visibly removed Himself from their midst. Moses was the only remaining point of contact for the grace of God in their lives. Only he now experienced the presence of God.

Verse 14 is best understood as a question, otherwise it merely repeats verse 17 and is confusing in the context. Accordingly, it should read: "Shall my presence go with you and shall I give you rest?"

The mediatorial role of Moses can be seen. He does exactly what God wanted him to do and what He had trained him for. We must not think that Moses was more lenient and gracious than God. For was it not God who had called Moses and who had patiently trained him?

Therefore, on the basis of Moses' arguments as a mediator and on the basis of the people's repentance and attitude of contrition, these were the progressive steps of mercy and favor witnessed by Israel. First, the Lord relented in the threatened judgment (32:14). Second, the people were allowed to continue on to Canaan with divine guidance, not the presence of the Lord Himself but that of a heavenly messenger (32:34; 33:1-2). Finally, the Lord Himself would once again accompany Israel on their journey to Canaan (33:15-17).

Israel learned that there is no substitute for the personal presence of the living God. How foolish and how risky it is for us to let sin interrupt and finally usurp that relationship. Let us therefore immediately implore the Savior for His forgiveness.

### WE RISK FACING THE LOSS OF THE GOODNESS OF GOD FOR OUR SIN (33:18—34:7)

Because God was pleased with Moses and because He knew him by name, God graciously acted favorably on his previous request. But Moses made yet another request of the Lord. He wanted to be shown His glory.

The glory of God is sometimes treated as a religious term whose meaning is better left unexplained. (It is often spoken with an odd inflection of the voice as it sort of rolls around in the speaker's mouth.) But the glory of God is nothing less than the sheer weight of His presence. At its root lies the concept of heaviness, and only in its secondary derivatives does it come to mean the out-splashing, or radiance, of God's glory.

Thus it happened that Moses witnessed in a new way all the goodness that is contained in the name of God. Moses was not allowed to look directly on God's face—no one could do that and live (33:20). But he was permitted to look on the aftereffects of the splendorous glory of God (33:23). The word is usually translated "back," but that is certainly inappropriate here. God is incorporeal and does not have any physical form as such (see Isa. 31:3 and John 4:24). However, the term can also refer to that which is behind or what comes after, and that is the rendering I prefer—a translation that readily suggests itself, especially in our space age with its rockets and their afterburners and afterglow. God caused all His "goodness," that is, all His attributes, to pass before His servant, plainly manifesting the sum and substance of what He is before the eyes of His servant. The aftereffect of the radiance was awesome.

Not only did God cause His goodness to pass by Moses, but He also proclaimed His "name." The name of God signifies more than the mere vocable or nomenclature by which He is addressed. The name in Scripture also signifies the person's character, attributes, and nature, the entirety of all that is connected with one's person. This may be seen in phrases like "to walk in the name of the Lord" or "taught them your name" found in certain ethical injunctions and doctrinal teachings. What could have been more comforting in this context of alienated sinners than the rehearsal of all that the divine name means over against the desperate needs of unrevived and ailing men and women? Thus the Lord passed by, and in august and stately terms He trumpeted forth: "Yahweh, Yahweh, the compassionate and gracious God, slow to anger and abounding in grace and truth" (34:6).

The name *Yahweh* (meaning," I am that I am") was in itself another declaration, not only of the aseity, or self-existence, of God, but more directly of the fact that He was God, *who would be there* to see, act, forgive, and do whatever needed to be done. This name He had patiently explained to Moses in Exodus 6:1-8. Now Moses was just grasping the full impact of what had been merely words.

Five special attributes of God are unfolded in this declaration of His name as He passed before Moses. First there was mercy or compassion. That is, at the head of the list of the divine perfections stood the benevolence of God. It is this attribute that predisposes our Lord toward us poor, miserable sinners, prompting Him to grant us relief, kindness, and clemency. No wonder the psalmist celebrates God as being plenteous in mercy. Connected with the noun for "womb," this word depicts the love of a mother for her baby. It is that same attribute that excited the apostle Paul in Ephesians 2:4-7, "But God, who is *rich in mercy*, for His great love wherein He loved us, even while we were dead in our sins, has made us alive." And likewise the apostle Peter raves, "Blessed be the God and Father of our Lord Jesus Christ, who, according to His *abundant mercy*, has begotten us again unto a living hope by the resurrection from the dead" (1 Pet. 1:3).

The second quality is the graciousness of God. How richly He has acted towards us, granting one unmerited gift after another, especially the gift of forgiveness and reconciliation.

He is, in the third place, "long of nostrils." This is an anthropomorphism, or description of God in the form of men. Just as anger tends to swell one's nostrils, so the opposite is evidenced here. Bush commented,

> Nothing is more wonderful than the patience of God when we consider the provocations which he continually receives at the hands of the ungodly. . . . Nay to bring the matter home to ourselves . . . [have] we not provoked him to anger every day of our lives? Yet to the praise of his patience here we still find ourselves, standing on praying ground, and favored with the offers and opportunities of pardon.[4]

The fourth and fifth attributes are treated together: "full of grace and truth." That is how John described Jesus in John 1:17, with a deliberate allusion to this statement of Yahweh in Exodus 34:6-7, a statement repeated some ten times in the Old Testament itself. The richness, plenteousness, and sheer bountifulness of His favor staggers the imagination, as does His unadulterated truth. Truth of every description must take its genesis in the source and Lord of all truth. Likewise, we would not have known grace, God's unmerited favor, unless it had been revealed in Him who so freely and bountifully forgave Israel of

4. Ibid., p. 245.

their outrageous actions, thoughts, and blasphemies in the treacherous incident of the golden calf.

By now God's invitation to us is abundantly clear. Why would anyone attempt to live with the guilt and despair of their sins? Why would we wish to risk so much for so little? Why would believers live like spiritual paupers and act with such mediocre results in their own churches and in the spread of the gospel around the world?

Revival would come to America, yes, to any nation of the world, if we obeyed the injunction of Scripture and confessed our sin. How foolishly Israel acted and how stupid she appeared when she did not quickly own up to her sin and seek the Lord's offer of forgiveness. Are we not equally foolish if we also refuse to repent? Look at what the name of God means once again, and claim each one of those five attributes for yourself. Enjoy the fullness of every bit of the goodness of God, for He delights to act on behalf of any and all who will take Him at His word. Let the great pardoning name of God pass before you and your house this day.

# 3

## It Is Time to Serve the Lord Only:

---

### REVIVAL UNDER SAMUEL
### 1 Samuel 7:1-13

It was time for revival once again. The state of both the religious and national life had slipped to a new low in the days of the judges of Israel. There had been at least five different respites from the dreary drone of wickedness and evil during those wretched days when "there was no king in Israel and every man did what was right in his or her own eyes" (Judg. 17:6; 18:1; 19:1; 21:25). But it is impossible from this distance to document whether a genuine revival took place during any of that period of time.

It is true, of course, that periodically Israel "cried out to the Lord" for deliverance, and He sent them a savior not once but repeatedly. But only in the last instance of this monotonous cycle is it recorded that Israel ever acknowledged their sin and bluntly confessed, "We have sinned against [Yahweh] because we have forsaken our God and have served the Baals" (Judg. 10:10). Again according to verse 15, "The people of Israel said to Yahweh, 'We have sinned; do to us whatever seems right to you; only deliver us we beg you.'"

Never is it recorded that there was any evidence of change on the part of the people, except for their prayers of desperation. The Hebrew word used for their prayer is connected with the word *cry,* and hence they were prayers born out of distress and deep despair. But they were without any apparent contrition or repentance or a solid renunciation of their former way of life. Accordingly, the spiritual tide had been running out for decades and centuries when God graciously raised up Samuel.

Rarely has immorality, injustice, and corruption of every sort achieved greater freedom. Samples of all of these sins could be found in the priest's own office and home. Eli had failed both as a leader of the nation and as a father. The offerings to the Lord were distorted, and Eli's sons exceeded every boundary of good taste, morality, and common decency. They insisted on having the sacrifice done to their specifications rather than God's (1 Sam. 2:12-17), and they brazenly "lay with the women who served at the entrance of the tent of meeting" (1 Sam. 2:22). Never once, however, did Eli attempt to restrain Hophni and Phineas, and for this ultimately he was rebuked by God (1 Sam. 3:13). Things indeed had become critical when the same evil that society was guilty of was also commonly reported in the household of faith. What then shall that nation or people plead in the day of God's wrath? This sign more than any other barometer of wickedness is the one that sounds the alarm, supposing there are any left who still have enough spiritual discernment to hear it.

But the litany of sins is longer than the few alluded to already. These were days in which "the Word of God was rare" (1 Sam. 3:1). As wickedness took hold of lives, the Word of God became proportionately scarce. This is another principle that the watchful observer of revivals must note. When pagans and believers alike find it convenient or preferable to substitute almost anything in place of the reading, hearing, and proclamation of the Word of God, beware: trouble for that people is just around the corner.

Not even the oppression of the Philistines had driven Israel to her senses. Nor had the loss of the nation's most sacred treasure caused concern among the people. For by now the Ark of the Covenant had been out of the center of Israel's religious life for twenty years, and no one seemed to be overly exercised about it or deeply concerned for its return. No, these were the worst of times for Israel, and the tragedy (as it usually is in such times and places) was that few knew it.

Suddenly there was a break in this boring and embarrassing downward march in spirituality. How it came about is not altogether clear. Certainly twenty long years of continual harassment and the frustration of frequent military incursions must have helped. One clue is given in the Hebrew text. It shows that verses 2 and 3 of 1 Samuel 7 are closely connected. There is no gap between them, for the action of the Hebrew infinitive translated "abode" or "remained" is continued in the five verbs associated with it somewhat as follows: "The ark remained at Kiriath Jearim, and it happened, and the days multiplied, and the days grew to twenty years, and all the house of Israel mourned, and then Samuel said. . ." That is, Israel had mourned a disproportionately long time. Misery had once again earned the first opportunity for the hearing of the Word of God in its rightful authenticity.

The focal point for 1 Samuel 7 seems to be located in verses 3 and 4. There the theme of *serving God only* appears twice: "Fix your hearts on the Lord and *serve Him only*" and "so the Israelites put away their Baals and Ashtaroth and *served the Lord only*." Moreover, the chapter contains three *challenges* from Samuel to Israel and by application to all who would, like Israel, also wish to be revived in their spiritual lives:

1. We must commit ourselves to the Lord (vv. 1-4).
2. We must confess our sin and pray to the Lord (vv. 5-9).
3. We must count on God's help and act boldly (vv. 10-13).

These challenges face all who hunger and thirst after righteousness.

## WE MUST COMMIT OURSELVES TO THE LORD (7:1-4)

Twenty years of uninterrupted oppression by the Philistines had humbled God's people. Misery had accomplished what blessing could not. Israel cried out to the Lord they had neglected.

The revival began as many revivals begin: with loud weeping and mournful lamentation over the heavy load of guilt and its effects. So it was, for example, in the revival of the Indians in the whole area of the Susquehanna under David Brainerd. As he commenced proclaiming the message "Herein is love," John Shearer reports that

> men fell at his feet in anguish of soul. These were men who could bear the most acute torture without flinching. But God's arrow had now pierced them; their pain could not be concealed and they cried out in their distress, "Have mercy on me." What impressed Brainerd most deeply was that though these people came to him in a multitude, each one was mourning apart. The prophecy of Zechariah was fulfilled before his eyes. The woods were filled with the sound of a great mourning.[1]

1. John Shearer, *Old Time Revivals: How the Fire of God Spread in Days Now Past and Gone* (London: Pickering and Inglis, n.d.), p. 43.

So it happened in Israel as well: "They lamented after God" (v. 2). Suddenly there had come a decided reorientation of the inner life of those who long had sensed no need of God. The pain and grief inflicted by the ruthless Philistine conquerors had done God's office work. "The image," says David Erdmann, describing the force of "lamented," "is that of a child that goes weeping after its father and mother, that it may be relieved of what hurts it."[2] It is a verb meaning "to wail, lament" (cf. Ezek. 32:18; Mic. 2:14), and it connotes sighing and heavy breathing.

But there was another strong force at work during those same twenty years, and all too many tend to overlook it, both in relation to those times and in the current setting. It was the preaching of God's faithful servant Samuel. Had not the text itself clearly anticipated this development? For in 1 Samuel 3:19 the writer remarks under the inspiration of God that "the Lord was with Samuel as he grew up, and he let none of His Word fall to the ground." Graciously God had anticipated the final crumbling of the dam. When the sighing broke out, there was the Word of God. It had been there all those twenty years, but the people could not hear it. Sin had deafened them to it. But the prophetic labors, like those of so many of God's present ministers of the Word, were rewarded after long years of waiting.

The prophet expressed himself conditionally. "If you are returning" (v. 3), he intoned. The participle "returning" assumes that the people had already started to turn inwardly towards the Lord. Thus the work of God was already underway. Accordingly, we are supplied the *context* (lamentation) for their hearing this word, the *means* (preaching) for this obedient response, and the *content* (what follows in v. 3*b*) of that word.

The first aspect of this word of the Lord was the same as that demanded of Jacob: "Get rid of your foreign gods" (Gen. 35:2; cf. also Josh. 24:23). A wholehearted fellowship with the living God is incompatible with any and all competing loyalties.

The second emphasis in Samuel's message from the Lord to Israel and to us is "Fix your hearts on God." If the preceding command was negative, this is the positive side of the same truth. An established, or fixed, heart is the opposite of a wavering, vacillating state of mind, which in ordinary circumstances often marks persons caught in the web of heavy grief and sighing. But here was a deliberate and solid

---

2. C. F. David Erdmann, *The Books of Samuel*, in Lange's Commentary on Holy Scripture (New York: Armstrong, 1877), p. 120.

decision to toss every other diversion away and to serve God alone.

The third and central theme of Samuel's message was to "serve Him only." It is not enough to empty our lives of all the false crutches and idols that we have brazenly erected there; we must also be willing to have this empty service replaced by glad service to the only true and living God. This again was another positive aspect of his message. And what a privilege to serve so exalted a friend as the Lord of glory.

One more aspect needed to be added, and this fourth element of Samuel's word was the promissory aspect of God's Word to all who from the heart will obey the living God. "He would deliver [them] out of the power of the Philistines" (v. 3c). Thus when we turn to God in true repentance, He then will turn to us, and He will remove the terrible source of our anguish. But it has to be carefully observed, yes, even for this Old Testament economy, that what was being asked for here was more than external showmanship or elaborate ritual. No, the response had to be "with all your hearts" (v. 3).

Who said Old Testament religion was more a matter of external religion? Those who take this line of reasoning have no idea what they are talking about. Prior to the Flood the Lord read the "thoughts of the hearts" of that wicked generation that had to be destroyed (Gen. 6:5). He is in the habit of "detecting the thought of the wicked" (Prov. 15:26), for "the Lord searches every heart and understands every motive behind the thoughts" (1 Chron. 28:9). Yes, "the Lord knows the thoughts of man" (Ps. 94:11). It ought to be abundantly clear from these samples representing some twenty-five Old Testament texts that a person's inner disposition and motives are clearly read by God. He personally holds us responsible for responding to Him with anything less than a total commitment of our inner beings for revival. The case was no different for Israel, for God was no different then than He is now. Thus the mighty preaching of Samuel set the tone, the agenda, and the conditions for a new work of God in their midst. But there is another challenge we must face.

## WE MUST CONFESS OUR SIN AND PRAY TO THE LORD (7:5-9)

It was time for a national assembly, for when the conditions are right a revival is inevitable. And all the elements for revival were now in place. Thus, just as atmospheric conditions signal the coming of the next weather system, so the earnestness, repentance, and removal of idols in Israel signaled the presence of the proper conditions for revival. It was in the hands of God as to when and if that revival would be granted.

The called assembly at Mizpah, then, was not the originating cause for the revival. Those conditions were spiritual in nature and had already taken place in the hearts of the people prior to this invitation. As Autrey observed, "It was not really a question of whether there would have been a revival if there had been no assemblage at Mizpeh [*sic*], but was it possible not to have a Mizpeh?"[3]

Mizpah, meaning "watchtower," has been identified with two sites. The first is with a site connected with the prophet Samuel's name known as Nabi Samwil. It is located just five miles northwest of Jerusalem in the tribe of Benjamin on a hill 2,935 feet high, overlooking the city. The other site is the northern extension of the Mount of Olives known today as Scopus, also meaning "watchman." Preference should be given to the former site, for it was also later honored as the place from which the war against Benjamin was launched (Judg. 20), where Saul was elected king (1 Sam. 10:17), and from which Judas Maccabaeus led his revolt against Antiochus Epiphanes.

To this place all Israel came. The time was ripe, and in the fullness of time God visited His people once again. Four things took place here that had a profound effect on Israel. First, there was an act of dedication. In Samuel's call for assembly, he had promised to intercede for the people at Mizpah. Let it be marked down as an extremely important principle that there can be no real, lasting work of God in revival without a genuine work of intercession on behalf of the people of God. Samuel was God's man who would stand in the gap and perform this ministry of a mediator. Verse 6 notes that after the people assembled, "they drew water and poured it out before the Lord." There is no parallel to this act in the Old Testament. The Targum renders this phrase paraphrastically, saying, "They poured out their hearts in repentance before the Lord." Apparently, the significance was that just as water poured out on the ground could not be collected again, so the commitment of their lives indicated a similar desire. But perhaps even more to the point was the later expression in Lamentations 2:19, "Pour out your heart like water," or the one in Psalm 22:15, "poured out like water." Surely this act signaled a deep contrition and humiliation for their sin. The water in this case may have reflected the tears, grief, and sorrow, the misery that their sins had caused them and for

---

3. C. E. Autrey, *Revivals of the Old Testament* (Grand Rapids: Zondervan, 1960), p. 53.

which they now were sorry. They wanted to dedicate themselves.

Next, there followed a self-imposed fast: their sorrow was more than just words; they backed it up with action. Thus they voluntarily afflicted their bodies to do without food in order to physically join in the grief of their souls. There was only one official day of fasting in Scripture (the one commanded for the day of atonement in Lev. 16:29, 31). Other days were acceptable, however, so long as they were not used as substitutes for doing the work of God or talismans for earning the favor of God when obvious acts of righteousness were being avoided, as was the case in Isaiah 58.

Verse 6 also says, in the third place, that they confessed, "We have sinned against the Lord." Because the area of their sin had been public, their confession had to be public, too, to be genuine. Accordingly, although two symbolic acts had set forth their grief over their sin, that is, the pouring out of water and the fasting, it was still necessary to acknowledge their repentance verbally. Of course the point is also well made that all sin is at once directed "against the Lord." Sin is a falling short of, a going beyond, or a straightforward violation of the command and/or Person of the living Lord. At its root it is opposition to the holy will of God. And this is what has blocked the relationship with God and separated all of us from His love and favor.

The fourth feature of the Mizpah meeting was that Samuel "judged Israel" (v. 6). Although some modern versions shy away from using this expression, it is clearly the meaning of the Hebrew. Perhaps we do not understand that there is a proper consequence for all genuine repentance. We thereby miss the fact that there must also be a work of adjudication to be carried out by God's earthly representative. Certainly God is the only one who can judge us in any real or ultimate sense, but He has also given us His representatives. Samuel was one such representative. He was there by God's design for the purpose of directing and ordering His people in the administration of justice and righteousness. In accordance with the previous acts of repentance, the reality of their confession must be tested, both the amount of restitution and the alacrity with which it was carried out. Wherever there had been theft, cheating, or other acts of injustice, the sincerity of the nation's confession was somewhat in doubt until there were acts of full restoration or plans for it. God had placed Samuel in the post of leader of this great convocation in order that he might exercise the function of "judging."

As Samuel had promised (v. 5), he also entered fully into the work of intercession on behalf of Israel. There is no greater work in a revival than the work and ministry of prayer. Without this most necessary petitioning of the Lord, revivals are dead before they get started. This is the universal testimony of all the revivals in the Bible and in history.

But Israel's concern was that Samuel might cease this ministry of praying on their behalf. Much is said these days about what goes into making a leader and what are good management principles. But few components of either can be as rudimentary for the would-be pastor, overseer, or leader in the church (or any other part of God's vineyard) than this one essential prerequisite of praying constantly and fervently for the people over whom God has graciously placed you. So Samuel prayed for all of them. It was the highest purpose he had in the gracious calling of God. He presented the people in prayer as objects of God's mercy, forgiveness, and grace.

But this is never the end of our prayers on behalf of the community of faith. There is always the matter of a right relationship to God and prayer for the growth in grace of these same people. Revival was meant to be a continual reviving of the life.

Mark it well: whenever there are deep stirrings of the Spirit of God in the renewing and reviving of lives, there the evil one will also be just as active in attempting to counter all the good work that has been done. His tricks are too many and varied to be listed here, but the people of God would be foolish to overlook them or to be ignorant of them. Accordingly, just as God was stirring the hearts of Israel at Mizpah, the devil was rousing a mistaken judgment among the Philistines: the Israelites had assembled at Mizpah in order to launch a national revolt against their rule over them.

When this became clear to Israel, they cried to Samuel, "Do not cease crying out to the Lord our God for us, that He might rescue us from the clutches of the Philistines" (v. 8). And there is our sin as leaders: often we fail our people by failing to pray for them. If there is any text that is needed for the revival of God's leaders, it is this one. God's work is not merely related to the quality and depth of the biblical exposition each week, the number of visits made to new families, the extensiveness of our counseling or discipleship programs, or any similar good and important works; it is most directly related to the quality, endurance, and earnestness of our daily petition to God on behalf of those whom we serve. May we not sin against God by failing to pray continually for His sheep.

Samuel, in his priestly function, presented the people to God in two ways: by prayer and by the sacrifice of a young (seven-day-old) lamb (see Lev. 22:27). The point is that prayer without a sacrifice is groundless. But thanks be to God that He has provided the final sacrifice that has opened the way into His presence in prayer for all who have accepted His free gift and sacrifice.

It should also be noted that this lamb was given up *wholly* as a whole burnt offering. It was a whole burnt offering because the people had resolved to give themselves fully and undividedly to the one who had graciously forgiven them and restored them to new life.

Verse 9 adds so beautifully, but in such stark simplicity: "And the Lord answered him." Later Jeremiah would learn the same lesson. "Call on Me and I will answer you and show you great and mighty things which you know not" (Jer. 33:3). What a challenge to confess our sins and to enter into prayer on behalf of God's people. When our hearts are loosed from all the junk that binds them and holds them captive, we experience unprecedented joy. Why should we who make up the church continue to allow lust to blind our eyes, greed for money and possessions to occupy our pursuits, and ambition to swallow up our hearts? Instead, let us confess our sin and be healed. Let us make full and fair restitution for all that we have taken. Let us enter into prayer for God's work, workers, and people, lest we sin further by failing to pray for one another. Only in so acting can we be prepared for the third challenge this text brings to us.

## WE MUST COUNT ON GOD'S HELP AND ACT BOLDLY (7:10-13)

If we are to serve God only, then we cannot look at circumstances with too much alarm. They will cripple and immobilize us spiritually, physically, and emotionally.

Thus it happened that God not only answered prayer when Israel decided to confess their sin and serve Him only, but He also began to work all things for good on their behalf. For just as the Philistines decided to attack them while they were still in the midst of their revival meetings at Mizpah, God dramatically intervened, striking the enemy with lightning from heaven. As the Philistines attempted to climb the heights of Mizpah, God sent loud thunder and threw the whole assault into disarray (v. 10). In that condition they were easily routed by God's men. In a similar way, God had worked for Joshua in the past (Josh. 10:10), and He will work again for the deliverance of all who call on His name, if they are walking in the light as He is in the light.

Because all of us are prone to forget those times when we were in deep trouble and how God has rescued us so wonderfully, it is altogether appropriate that we set up certain memorials to aid our frail memories. So Samuel set up a stone and named it *Ebenezer,* meaning "stone of help" (v. 12). God had helped them when they no more deserved to be helped than we often deserve. But it was also meant to be an encouragement for the new trials of tomorrow. There is nothing to fear when we walk by faith, conscious that our sins have been forgiven and that we serve the Lord alone.

The good word that Samuel uttered on this occasion was, "Up to this point the Lord has helped us" (v. 12). That demarcation embraced not only all the victories they had experienced in the past but also the sorrows and defeats as well. How patient a teacher our Lord is. Twenty years of waiting (until Israel finally sensed what their Lord knew from the very beginning) had come to fruition. The result was indeed lasting, for no longer did the Philistines come into Israel's territory as victors. Repeatedly they were repulsed. And this was because of the positive effects of the revival and the prayers of God's servant Samuel. Notice that verse 13*b* indicates that the staying of the Philistines continued for as long as Samuel lived. Who could miss the connection between the people's request that Samuel should never cease to pray for them and the winning ways of Israel?

Thus a nation was reborn and unified in the joyful service of God. Where there had been division, strife, fruitlessness, and guilt-laden lives, there now was happy service for the living God.

To serve God alone, therefore, is to make Him sole Lord. It is to recognize and serve no other master or rival. With a heart fixed unreservedly on Him, all forms of vacillation, ambivalence, and doublemindedness are utterly rejected and repented of. We must choose this day whom we will serve, just as Joshua declared he would (Josh. 24:15). And it is time we also confessed with Israel of old and the hymn writer:

> Here I raise my Ebenezer,
> Hither by thy help I've come;
> And I hope by Thy good pleasure,
> Safely to arrive at home.

Has it not been too long since we last saw the fires of genuine, nation-wide revival sweep our land? Have we not sensed a yearning for authenticity and whole-hearted service for the living God that is devoid of staleness, boredom, and lack-luster dullness? It is time for revival to begin in the house of God. The spiritual state of the church is mixed today, but if a generalization may be permitted, in proportion to our numbers the church has been outclassed when it comes to general effectiveness and the production of lasting results. Few in society, government, or crime fear our prayers or sense the dynamic power of the resurrection to the degree they should. Is this not a distressing signal that revival is needed?

May the Lord of the church come and revive His church again and call each of His own to a new basis for serving Him only.

# 4

# It Is Time to Let God Be God:

## REVIVAL UNDER ELIJAH
## 1 Kings 18

Fifty-eight years had passed since the kingdom was ripped apart in 931 B.C. At that time the glorious united kingdom, which had lasted for well nigh a full century with all the splendor of the reigns of David and Solomon, was divided into two southern and ten northern tribes. Subsequently things had not gone all that well, especially for the northern ten tribes.

During this relatively brief time, the northern tribes had been ruled over by seven kings: Jeroboam, the installer of the two calves designed to replace the worship of Yahweh (1 Kings 12:28-32); Nadab, who walked in the sins of his father, Jeroboam (1 Kings 15:22); Baasha, who murdered Nadab (1 Kings 15:27); Elah, a drunkard and murderer (1 Kings 16:8-9); Zimri, who was guilty of treason (1 Kings 16:20); Omri, a military adventurer who did "worse than all who were before him" (1 Kings 16:25-26); and finally Omri's son, Ahab, who did more evil than all who were before him. It was Ahab who married the infamous Jezebel, daughter of the king of Sidon (1 Kings 16:30-31). These were not the best of times politically. Neither were they the best of times spiritually, for the nation had been won over to the worship of the Canaanite gods, especially Baal. The decline of national and spiritual strength was enough to make any God-fearing person weep. But where was that remnant?

Elisha raised that same question after the prophet Elijah had been taken up to glory: "Where now is the Lord God of Elijah?" (2 Kings 2:14). If ever the nation needed God, it was during these wretched days. Everything was turning to dust right in front of their eyes.

We cannot help agreeing with the significance of this question, not only for that day but for our day as well. How did God became so small in our eyes and in the eyes of our generation? Only lilliputian minds and hearts would have diminished God to the infinitesimal categories He is often relegated to by contemporaries. Is it any wonder that J. B. Philips wrote *Your God Is Too Small?*

Here is a crime that shouts to heaven for relief. We must beg God for pardon and for a new sense of His greatness. How dare we compare Him to men, forces, nations, problems, issues, or systems of our own invention? The shout of Isaiah must also be heard by our generation: "Say to the cities [of America, indeed of the world], 'Behold your God'" (Isa. 40:9). We need a whole new view of the living God in all His fullness as the only proper antidote for our poor emaciated categories in which we so pietistically but incorrectly operate.

In order to startle Israel back into the realities of thinking biblically about God, the Lord of glory sent a man, Elijah the Tishbite from Gilead. Few could have come from more lowly backgrounds than this man. Gilead was a high, stony region in Transjordan just east of the Sea of Galilee. Furthermore, Elijah was a nobody. Indeed, the only fact that we know about him is the name his parents seemed to have given him, meaning "Yahweh is my God."

Thus, while a nation was going crazy after a nonexisting god named Baal, this man by his very name shouted the reverse to the general eddies of his day. Almost out of nowhere he appeared and took the center of the stage in the palace of Ahab, that henpecked husband and poor excuse for a king. Without fanfare or wasted motion, he bravely announced to the weak Ahab, "As the Lord, the God of Israel, lives, in whose presence I stand, there shall not be dew or rain these next few years except by my word" (1 Kings 17:1). But how could this backwoods rustic fail to be impressed by the presence of royalty and all the splendors and pageantry of the Israelite court? Why was he more impressed with the presence of God than he was with being in the presence of the earthly monarch?

It would appear that Elijah possessed a vision of God that exceeded all the trappings of mortals. And that is the vision we will need to recapture if we are to experience the reviving power of God once again.

Yes, it is high time that we in our day let God be God.

In this the fourth great revival in the Old Testament (1 Kings 18), there are three *works* of God that demonstrate that He is the incomparable God:

1. He makes us courageous (vv. 1-20).
2. He shows us His power (vv. 21-40).
3. He answers our prayers (vv. 41-46).

In order to capture the attention of a people that had abandoned its exclusive loyalty to their Lord, God removed from them some of the assumed gifts of life. It is only God who can give or withhold rain. And that is what He did in this instance in order to pull men and women back to their senses once again.

## He Makes Us Courageous (18:1-20)

God's second command to His brave new recruit was suddenly given after three and a half years of absolute drought in which there was neither dew or rain. "Go," He commanded, "and present yourself before Ahab, and then I will send rain" (1 Kings 18:1). We are told, "So Elijah went."

How did Elijah become so bold? Did he not have any sense of self-protection, any desire to live? Had he not heard that Queen Jezebel was putting the Lord's prophets to death by the score? Was he not aware there was a price on his own head, so much so that every neighboring monarch had to swear to Ahab that they had not seen this elusive prophet or given him sanctuary?

It was God, of course, who made His servant so bold. Indeed, it is amusing to note with Arthur Pink that "wicked men are generally great cowards: their own consciences are their accusers, and often cause many misgivings when in the presence of God's faithful servants even though [these servants] occupy an inferior position in life to themselves."[1] There are many illustrations of this truth. "Herod feared John, knowing that he was a just and holy man" (Mark 6:20), and "Felix trembled before Paul" (Acts 24:25). Only the Lord can make us bold and courageous, even when we are facing powerful enemies.

For three and one-half years God tried to let the events of life, especially the awful suffering of the drought, soften the hearts of this royal

1. A. W. Pink, *The Life of Elijah* (London: Banner of Truth, 1963), p. 109.

couple along with their people. However, the reverse had happened. The queen was infuriated to such an extent that she took up killing the prophets of Yahweh as a hobby.

Yet God graciously sent His prophet back to the king. It is interesting that God asked Elijah first to obey by giving an announcement to the throne, and only then would He send rain. The correct rendering of these clauses seems to be "Go . . . and *then* I will send rain." How important those first steps of obedience are for the great and climactic moments of success later on.

Thus it came about "in the third year" that God finally was ready to confront His people with their serious vacillations and to place the option of a revival in front of them. It is true that Luke 4:25 and James 5:17 both say the drought lasted for three and a half years. But it might well have been that the prediction of 1 Kings 17:1 came six months after the first normal dry season. Josephus reported a severe drought under the Syrian king Ithobal, usually considered to be a contemporary of Ahab, for the lack of any rain or dew was area wide and therefore affected the neighboring countries as well.[2] It must have been embarrassing for Ahab to acknowledge to these kings that the reason for the drought was because of his nation's sin against the God of heaven and earth according to the declaration of one of his prophets named Elijah.

But it is also most disappointing to see how slow they were to respond to this act of severe love. As Jeremiah put it later on, "You, O Lord, struck them, but they were not grieved; you crushed them, but they refused correction; they have made their faces harder than stone and refused to repent" (Jer. 5:3). Probably some were more disposed to write the whole tragedy off as a freak event in nature than to see in it the divine hand of judgment. A spirit of hardness and defiance had counseled the people to stick it out, for it had to start raining soon. It could not go on like this forever.

Elijah was not only bold in facing the enemy, he was courageous in rebuking fellow believers as well (vv. 3-15). The believer we have in mind here is Obadiah, Ahab's "secretary of state." We are told straight out that Obadiah was a devout believer, for he "feared God greatly" (v. 3). Nor can he be faulted for holding a position of influence in a corrupt government, so long as it did not lead him to personally compromise his own principles. On the contrary, he could offer valuable ser-

---

2. Josephus *Antiquities* 8.13.2.

vice to Yahweh in this office, as in fact he did. Still many commentators complain that he was a compromiser and therefore out of the will of God at this time. Some will accuse him of these types of faults: (1) he gave no evidence of delight in seeing a fellow believer; (2) he resented being told to go tell Ahab that Elijah had returned; (3) he was self-centered and concerned only for his own protection and not for the welfare of the kingdom of God; (4) he distrusted Yahweh's words and rather feared that God would take Elijah away by the help of the Spirit of God; (5) he is overly defensive about his actions from his youth on and wishes to brag about his rescue mission for the only hundred prophets of Yahweh.

Now there is no doubt that Obadiah was fearful, but so is the prophet Habakkuk in the midst of his own turmoil of soul in Habakkuk 3. But we cannot agree that Obadiah gave any evidence of compromising, for verses 3 and 12 contradict that view. His reference to his daring deeds was not a boast but was rather a means of attesting his sincerity. Nevertheless, Obadiah still needed a gentle rebuke from the prophet Elijah. Elijah settled all of Obadiah's fears with a strong declaration in the name of the Lord (v. 15). And so Obadiah obeyed willingly without any further debate. The prophet's word was as certain as the fact that the Lord of hosts was living.

But the Lord also empowered His servant Elijah to rebuke the wicked (vv. 17-20). At last the long-sought confrontation was taking place. The first words out of Ahab's mouth were to shift the blame from himself to God's messenger. Indeed, how quick the wicked are to distort the facts and to foist the burden for the state of things that have obviously gone sour onto the shoulders of those who merely announce or proclaim the divine judgment for these sins.

The gods of Ahab and Jezebel specialized in rain, dew, and thunder. Yet they had not raised even a peep in all the three years since Elijah had announced to Ahab the awful news that Yahweh would send drought, Baal or no Baal. The smarting hearts of this royal duo saw that their only defense was to rouse sympathy for themselves and to shift the blame onto God's minister. Why could they not see that these were just games they were playing?

God's servant was once again more than a ready match for this weak defense: "I have not made trouble for Israel, but you and your father's family have" (v. 18). And the root of the problem was not to be found in the symptoms but rather in the real cause: "You have abandoned the Lord's commands and have followed Baals" (v. 18).

Obviously Ahab was in no position to complain, protest, or bargain. The real person in charge now was God's man. Therefore, in a most extraordinary move *he* ordered the king to summon all of Israel to Mt. Carmel for a showdown. The state-paid 450 prophets of Baal and the 400 prophets of Asherah were likewise to appear. What could Ahab do? I wonder if he even dared to tell Jezebel what he had been ordered to do, for her absence is conspicuously noticeable. So Ahab sent word out to all Israel to gather at the assigned place (vv. 19-20).

How marvelous are the works of God through the intrepid Tishbite. But this was only the beginning, for God had an even greater work in store for all those despisers of genuine religion.

### HE SHOWS US HIS POWER (18:21-40)

If there ever was a lonely man in the history of faith, Elijah was that man. But one person plus God is always a majority, and Elijah believed that implicitly. His view of God had been forged and strengthened during those long days at the brook Cherith, penned up with no place to go, and then in a suburb of Sidon named Zarephath, the very backyard of the Gentile queen, Jezebel. Three years of prayer and meditation on the Word of God were no small part in the preparation of this prophet for one grand afternoon of work. But we must be careful not to think that it all happened spontaneously, without any agonizing of heart or soul. That is a very narrow view of spiritual preparation.

Immediately, without any wavering or waffling of position, Elijah seized the initiative and bluntly challenged the people with this question: "How long will you limp [waver, totter] between two opinions? If Yahweh is God, follow him" (v. 21). The word "limp" is the famous word used of the Passover. It refers to people who are not walking uprightly but who are like intoxicated persons. That is, the people were fickle, inconstant, and broadly syncretistic in their faith. Moreover, the people were double-minded, fence sitters who wanted to retain full loyalties to two opposing opinions, two parties, and two minds at the same time. They were like the Republicans in 1884 who were humorously called mugwumps because they, too, like Israel and many candidates for revival today, had their mugs (i.e., faces) on one side of the fence and their "wumps" (i.e., the seats of their trousers) on the other. God, however, "hates double-minded persons" (Ps. 119:113).

Who then was on the Lord's side, clearly and without any equivocation? asks our text, even as Moses had asked during the golden calf episode recounted in Exodus 32:26. Jesus warned that "he that is not with me is against me" (Matt. 12:30) and that if we were neither hot nor cold, He would spit us out of His mouth (Rev. 3:15).

What does a person say to this? What is there to say when the Word of God unmasks us for what we are? The Israelites did what we need to do as well; they "said nothing" (v. 21). "O for that plain and faithful preaching," exclaimed A. W. Pink, "which would so reveal to men the unreasonableness of their position . . . that every objection would be silenced and they would stand self-condemned."[3] The power of God had certainly demonstrated itself in the challenge of Elijah. But the most awesome display of the power of God was yet to come.

The choice of fire to evidence the power and authenticity of the claims of God is in itself a study in theology. Surely when the land, beasts, and all humanity were languishing, the answering of their prayers with rain rather than fire might seem much more appropriate. But God had Elijah choose fire both to show His power and His acceptance of the sacrifice. On three previous occasions God had sent fire from the heavens to light the fires under a sacrifice. The first was at the dedication of the altar of the Tabernacle in Leviticus 9:24, the second when David dedicated the altar on the future site of the Temple in 1 Chronicles 21:26, and the third when Solomon dedicated the newly built Temple in 2 Chronicles 7:1. On each of these occasions, God's fire marked His acceptance and approval of the sacrifice offered. The theological point, then, is this: before the mercy and favor of the rains can return to the drought stricken landscape, there must intervene a sacrifice, a substitute for sin, that is acceptable to God. No reconciliation is possible, nor can things return to normal, without the intervention and divine acceptance of a substitute to bear the penalty of the separated people.

With the appearance of fire often also came the revelation of the divine name (e.g., Ex. 3:15). It was, in fact, a declaration of the glory of God and His presence, even as it was at the burning bush (Ex. 3:2). Even the restoration of the altar by Elijah had theological significance, for he took twelve stones, not the politically safe ten representing the ten northern tribes of his nation, and deliberately alluded to a similar situation in the history of Israel when Jacob and his family of twelve sons had to be called back from idolatry. As Elijah challenged the idolaters here to get rid of their false gods, so had Jacob in an earlier

3. Pink, p. 127.

revival in Genesis 35. The informing theology was obvious, and his refusal to legitimize the nation's sinful division into ten and two tribes for these fifty-eight years was also pointedly clear. Elijah, as the expression goes, had a lot of skin on his nose. Or was he just functioning with the boldness of an accredited messenger of Yahweh?

What took place as Elijah allowed the Baal contingency to go first is at once both humorous and pitiable. From six in the morning until three o'clock in the afternoon these devotees cried, shouted, and cut themselves with swords and knives, all to no avail. Meanwhile, Elijah rested on the mountainside, perhaps staring down at the Mediterranean Sea and thoughtfully chewing on a piece of straw. (The text does not tell us that he did these things; but it says so in the margins of my Bible. I must warn the reader, however; there are very wide margins in my Bible, and the notes I put there are *perspired*: only what is in the text of Scripture is *inspired*.)

If you were ever tempted to laugh out loud while reading the Bible, here is one of the places you might wish to do so. How sincere and yet how pathetic and misdirected was the worship and the prayers of these prophets. Elijah decided to have a little fun and offered some free advice as to how they might get a response, as if he were in sympathy with them or in hope that they might be able to call down fire. The truth of the matter was that he knew there was no chance at all for them to succeed. So Elijah mockingly suggested that they might wish to shout louder (v. 27)—it is reported in the Canaanite religious tablets discovered at Ugarit that Baal sometimes went on trips and also frequently took naps. Indeed, Baal might even be (how shall we say this delicately?)—rather indisposed and unable to come to the telephone at this minute. And these stupid fools took the advice seriously and increased their frantic activity, hoping to attract Baal's deaf ear. But should they not have known? Was it not clear to them that the Lord, the God of Israel, was God and there never was and never would be any other competing God anywhere in the whole of creation? And if Baal was the god of dew, rain, and thunder, why had he not shown his stuff prior to this? There had been three years for him to counter the Lord's judgment on the lands of the Middle East, but not once did he send a drop of moisture. That should have said it all. But how slow we humans are to get the point.

Now at exactly the time when the evening sacrifice would be offered at the Temple in Jerusalem, where the two southern tribes worshiped, Elijah began the service for sacrifice on the twelve-stone altar (vv. 30-

31). By so doing, he again reminded northern Israel of her original position before God. He also specifically referred to the previous revival (under Samuel) and attempted to awaken in their memories an earlier occasion when they had to be rebuked by God for the same thing. Again using the informing theology of Genesis 35, he said, "Your name shall be Israel." So their very name was based on the occasion when God had cleansed His people of their sin and had renamed them in the earliest revival recorded in the Old Testament.

Elijah's prayer was a masterpiece in simplicity and directness. In approximately sixty words in the original text, he appealed to the God of Abraham, Isaac, and Jacob to let it be known on that day that He was God and that there was no other (vv. 36-37). There was no need for a wearisome or drawn-out prayer. He had fervently prayed in his closet for over three years now.

Verse 38 bursts on the page of Scripture with the joy characteristic of the mighty God of the resurrection: "Then the fire of the Lord fell." This was no ordinary fire. For those who wish to speculate that it was the result of spontaneous combustion, traceable perhaps to the sword dances of the Baal dervishes, there are the three drenchings that the altar, the wood, the sacrifice, the stones, and the surrounding ditch received. And if it be protested further that this is an impossible feature to the story because there was supposed to be a shortage of water, I merely point out that there was plenty of salt water at the base of Mt. Carmel. How glad I am that God led Elijah to take these additional steps, almost in anticipation of our modern skeptical age. It surely has saved us from reading and responding to some two dozen doctoral theses advocating some variation on the spontaneous combustion theory as a result of the hobgoblin prancings about of these masochistic prophets in their weapons dance.

And was there revival? Were the people convinced? Verse 39 affirms that "when the people saw this, they fell prostrate." I think I would, too, if I had been there and had witnessed such a mighty display of the presence and power of God. Indeed it is a fearful thing to fall into the hands of the living God if we are not prepared to meet Him. And Israel certainly was not prepared to meet Him. They had acted as if He were merely one more god on the god-shelf along with the others. But now the people's spontaneous declaration was "Yahweh, He is God; Yahweh, He is God." (v. 39). And so He is, without any rival at all. Why are we forever trying even today to demote Him and to place other loyalties alongside of Him?

## HE ANSWERS OUR PRAYERS (18:40-46)

The final work of God observed in this chapter is that evidenced in answering prayer. If we have seen Elijah in public prayer on the top of Mt. Carmel, we are now given a view of his ministry in private prayer in the closet.

It is no wonder that Scripture uses Elijah as an example of prayer in James 5:17-18. "Elijah," James assures us, "was a mortal just like us. He prayed earnestly that it should not rain, and it did not rain on the land for three and one-half years. He prayed again and the heavens gave rain, and the earth produced its crops." What a great encouragement to pray, and what a great encouragement to come to God to be revived again.

This portion of Scripture can be very helpful in teaching us what to pray for in revival and how to pray for it. Some have erroneously remarked that if God wishes to do something, it is none of our business. He probably does not need us interfering with His plans, so why should we pray? (This argument is especially convincing when it would appear that God has promised a certain outcome.) Again, if God needs any assistance, it is objected, why would He ask us merely to pray? But the promises of God were not meant to inhibit or to discourage us from praying. The plan of God is just 180 degrees opposite of that kind of thinking. This is reinforced when we compare verse 1 of chapter 18 with verses 42-44. Had not God promised Elijah that if he would go and announce His message to Ahab, He in turn would send rain? In fact we translated it as a result, or purpose, clause: "Go and present yourself . . . so that I may [or, *and then I will*] send rain" (v. 1). And so Elijah, fully persuaded of the fact that rain would come, nevertheless went to God in fervent, private prayer.

Too frequently we moderns have hidden behind the doctrine of the sovereignty of God as the reason we are hesitant to pray fervently and persistently for revival. Scripture will not tolerate such a conclusion any more than Elijah just sat and waited after the great immediate crisis was over. May Elijah's example (and remember, he is cited as our model of proper prayer technique in James) rebuke our poor excuses, and may we be taught that the promise of revival and showers of blessing in the good providence of God were not meant to say that we have no part or responsibility in this work.

We must note the following characteristics of Elijah's private prayers. First, he withdrew from the crowd and went into the privacy of his own thoughts with God in order to petition Him for what He had promised to do. Second, he prostrated himself in prayer before God, for he bowed his head between his knees, demonstrating in his body the state of his heart and soul. Of course there is no preferred or recommended posture for prayer in the Bible, but it is always proper for the whole person to enter into prayer, if it is to be a Spirit-led exercise of the whole person. Third, he was persistent in prayer, for he sent not just once but seven times to see if the answer was on the way. Fourth, he was fully confident and expectant that God would answer his prayer. Finally, he based his prayer, as we have already argued, on the promises of God.

Each aspect of this truth teaches us that God is God and that He delights in answering prayer. This work of God is just as significant in His work of making us bold or of showing us His power.

Our conclusion must be one of renewed admiration for the fact that God is the only Lord of history. The truth that Israel should have realized in that moment of great disclosure is that the Lord is God and there is no one like Him in all the universe.

How shameful Israel must have felt. How cheap they must have seemed when the prophets of Baal failed so dramatically and so miserably. But then, how can we in our generation throw stones and criticize them? Have we not been just as guilty of substituting all sorts of schemes, programs, personalities, and prior commitments in the place that should be rightfully occupied by God alone? Is it not time that we, too, came to know that God is God? Why have we likened Him so much to that which is unreal, false, and ephemeral?

Surely we are ripe candidates for revival when there is competition for the attention and support of God's people on Sundays by such things as national football games televised during church services or Superbowl Sunday in January. There is nothing wrong with legitimate leisure activities, such as times of pleasure at the symphony. But how the people of God complain when the allotted sixty minutes for worship is exceeded. One would never believe that these are the same people who will sit for hours on hard bleachers without backs to watch a ball game or who will clap for four encores at the musical event of the year. The contrast in our attitudes shouts to high heaven that we, too, need to come to know what it means to come face to face with the living God.

May God bring us a new vision of Himself and of the majesty of His person. Let us be done with artificial and inauthentic representations of God. And may He revive our hearts even as He did for Israel in Elijah's day.

# 5

## It Is Time to Seek the Lord:

---

### REVIVAL UNDER ASA
### 2 Chronicles 14-16

**G**od is not limited. He can work in all times, and the revival under the Judean king Asa proves that He can work in times of prosperity as well as adversity. In the fifteenth year of this monarch a great revival took place, but it was certainly different from any that we have investigated thus far in the Old Testament. Ernest Baker pinpointed that difference this way,

> It did not follow a period of religious decline, but a period of reformation. Neither was it occasioned by national adversity, causing the people in despair to turn to God; but it came after a season of increase and prosperity; and after a great national victory and deliverance. During the two preceding reigns, the worship of Yahweh had been pushed into the background, and the erection of idols and places for their worship had proceeded with the active support of the rulers. Upon Asa's accession to the throne, ecclesiastical reform was immediately effected. The state policy was reversed. The people were commanded to observe the law of God, and an active campaign against idolatry was instituted.[1]

In the majority of the revivals in history, it takes tragedy to finally arrest the attention of an apostatizing people of God, but in this case

---

1. Ernest Baker, *The Revivals of the Bible* (Capetown, South Africa: Miller, 1906), p. 37.

the background for the revival was a reformation. Instead of a time of spiritual dearth and religious decline, we are given a surprising exception in the revival under King Asa.

Now a reformation must not be confused with a revival. Reform may begin when God's Word forms the basis for all action, thinking, and living. It leads to a time of moral living and righteousness in the land. But revival begins in the heart and leads to deep contrition and repentance for sin, with a willingness to change, make restitution, and live differently from that time forward.

The reform movement of the king Asa continued for fifteen years before revival came. That would place the Judean revival prior to Elijah's in the northern kingdom twenty-five years later. Asa's revival occurred thirty-five years after the collapse of the united kingdom at the death of Solomon.

During the reformation period, however, Asa was actively pursuing all that was good and right in the sight of God (2 Chron. 14:2). He energetically assailed all pagan idolatry with a vengeance. Down came the foreign altar installations, sacred stones, and enigmatic cultic Asherah poles (vv. 3-4). The land also experienced a time of unusual prosperity. There was a tremendous amount of building going on. Asa put up walls, towers, bars, and gates and secured the land on every side (vv. 6-7). Towns were remodeled and repaired, and public works were promoted.

Generally, it is said that cycles of prosperity follow rather than precede revivals. But again, the Asa revival is an exception to this observation. It is not always necessary for God to send trouble to get our attention. Sometimes His very goodness forces us to realize that we are the recipients of abundant favor that we do not deserve. In times like these we are ripe for the persuasive work of God's gracious Holy Spirit.

America may be experiencing one of these eras of reformation. Although there are plenty of reasons for decrying the growth of wickedness, evil, and injustice at almost every level of our society, there is also a more positive side. For example, just a few years ago hardly any one spoke out against the terrible crime of abortion. Now both the executive branch of our government and our evangelical churches have closed ranks in an unprecedented way to forge one of the strongest alliances for righteousness this country has witnessed in years. Still, one swallow is not enough to declare that summer has arrived. However, there are other indicators as well. A whole host of social and moral crimes are under serious attack by these and other groups.

Among them are child abuse, wife beating, pornography, drunkenness, gambling, and war. Seldom has this writer seen such a rallying of the forces of good. Furthermore, according to reliable estimates, more than twenty-five percent of America's college and university students claim to be born-again believers. This is something like 2 1/2 million believers out of a total student population of 11 1/2 million. In the gracious providence of God, could it be that we are in the vanguard of a revival that God would grant if we who know Christ would only go further and meet the conditions? Our prayer is that this reformation might be strengthened in its depth, fervor, and effectiveness and that it would eventually, but quickly, lead to a full blown revival.

One other factor that led to revival in Asa's day should be noted here. During the fifteen years of his reformation, Asa had been equipping the army for any exigency. But when the challenge came, in the threat posed by Zerah from Ethiopia, he was vastly outnumbered. However, Asa gamely called on the name of the Lord and stated flatly that he relied on the Lord and on His name to extricate Judah from this ominous circumstance. And God granted a national victory in the face of overwhelming odds, which ordinarily would have signaled certain defeat. But it was this victory that God used to once again show how His goodness leads us to repentance (Rom. 2:4) and, in this case, revival.

Therefore, the key to Asa's importance is to be found in a single phrase: he sought the Lord. Thus in the three chapters (forty-eight verses; the parallel account in 1 Kings 15:9-24 has only fifteen) dedicated to his life in 2 Chronicles, the writer used the verb "to seek [the Lord]" nine times (14:4, 7 [twice]; 15:2, 4, 12, 13, 15; 16:12), showing that he meant it to be used paradigmatically. This is especially significant in light of the occurrence of the verb in 2 Chronicles 6-7. In the Introduction to this book it was pointed out that four verbs from chapters 6 and 7 form the programmatic outline for 2 Chronicles. That is, nearly one-half of the thirty-six chapters of 2 Chronicles are occupied with the five reigns that exhibited some of the greatest revivals in history, and each of these five accounts seems to focus on one of the four verbs mentioned. The first and the fifth account share the same verb, and this serves to form a sort of bracketing or framing of the argument.

It is true that "to seek" God is a favorite expression of the writer of Chronicles. He used it twenty-nine times altogether, whereas the parallel accounts in the books of Samuel and Kings used it only twice. The contrast can be seen by comparing 2 Chronicles 7:12-14, our controlling text in this study of revivals, with 1 Kings 9:2-3:

| *2 Chronicles 7:12-14* | *1 Kings 9:2-3* |
|---|---|
| The Lord appeared to Solomon in the night and said to him: | . . . the Lord appeared to Solomon a second time, as He had appeared to him at Gibeon. And the Lord said to him, "I have |
| "I have heard your prayer, and have chosen this place for myself as a house of sacrifice. When I shut up the heavens so that there is no rain, or command the locust to devour the land, or send pestilence among my people, if my people who are called by my name will humble themselves, and pray, and *seek my face*, and turn from their wicked ways, then I will hear from heaven, and will forgive their sin and heal their land. | heard your prayer and your supplication, which you have made before me." |

From this point on the Kings' material resumes and parallels Chronicles word for word.

But though the words "seek," "pray," "humble yourselves," and "turn" can be found in the speeches, prayers, and narratives of Chronicles, they particularly abound in the material that reports the five revivals that highlight this book. Therefore, this section, especially the description for the way to get back to fellowship with the living God, was indeed programmatic.

Within thirty-five years of the division of the kingdom, and as we have said, almost twenty-five years before God sent Elijah to the northern ten tribes, God had sent three prophets. They were Shemaiah (12:5, 7-8), Azariah (15:2-7), and Hanani (16:7-9). Shemaiah, of course, was earlier and ministered to King Rehoboam. He stressed the word "Humble yourself" (12:6, 7 [twice], 12). Next, Azariah stressed the theme of Asa's day, "Seek the Lord." Finally, Hanani expressed the same truth in another word, "Rely on the Lord" (16:7 [twice], 8).

Thus this episode announces to present day readers that it is time for us to seek the Lord. There are three *results* that we will experience if we are willing to do that:

1. We will experience a time of peace (14:2-7).
2. We will experience God's presence again (15:2-7).
3. We will prevail over our foes (14:9-15; 16:1-10).

Let us turn to see what these three results of seeking the Lord are and what it means to seek Him.

## WE WILL EXPERIENCE A TIME OF PEACE (14:2-7)

The prophet Shemaiah had set the stage for this section of the text. He warned Judah's first king following the rupture of the kingdom in 931 B.C. that because the king had abandoned God, God would abandon him (12:5). That sobered the king, and the text says repeatedly that he humbled himself (12:6, 7 [twice], 12). There was more going on here than meets the English reader's eye, however, for the Hebrew text has a word play going on between the term for "humble oneself" and the term for "subdue" (13:18).

Of the thirty-six times the term that lies behind this word play is found in the Old Testament, eighteen of them are found in Chronicles, and of those eighteen, fourteen are used in a religious sense. But it is the appearance of this term in its religious sense in 2 Chronicles 7:14 that sets the pattern and the program for the rest of the book of Chronicles and for a significant theology of revival.

When we come to Asa's day, we find that a reformation is under way, even though it is not a revival. Already some of the good benefits of what God was going to do were being realized. For here was a man who commanded Judah to seek the Lord, the God of their fathers, and to obey His laws and commands. (14:4).

What does it mean to seek the Lord? What it did not mean is seen in Leviticus 19:31, that is, to seek out mediums or wizards and to be defiled by them. But positively, it did mean to "seek the Lord and His strength, and His presence continually" (1 Chron. 16:11/Ps. 105:4). To "seek God" and to "seek His face" probably meant the same thing, unless the later expression had more of the nuance of searching for the companionship and comfort of His presence continually.[2]

2. "Seeking the face of the Lord" appears in 1 Chron. 16:11/Ps. 105:4; Ps. 24:6; 27:8 (twice); Hos. 5:15; 2 Sam. 21:1; and 2 Chron. 7:14. The more general statements of seeking the Lord are found in Ex. 33:7; Deut. 4:29; 2 Sam. 12:16; Ps. 40:17; 69:7; 70:5; Prov. 28:5; Isa. 51:1; Jer. 29:13; 50:4; Hos. 3:5; 5:6; 7:10; Dan. 9:3; Zeph. 1:6; Zech. 8:21; Mal. 3:1; Ezra 8:22; and the references in 1 Chron. 16:10/Ps. 105:3; and 2 Chron. 11:16; 15:4, 15; 20:4.

"Seeking Yahweh" can be used to define who is qualified to be a true member of the community of faith. "Not seeking Yahweh" disqualifies a person from full fellowship or any participation in that community. But if one is to judge by the words with which this expression is paired, seeking involves "knowing," "serving," and "being found by" God. Indeed, "the idea of 'seeking God' is so complex and so general in the Chronicler's Historical Work that one must consider the possibility that when all is said and done it denotes nothing other than the Chronicler's typical ideal of piety."[3]

In its prophetic use, the expression appears to be equivalent to a summons to repentance. Thus, Amos 5:4-6 urges, "Seek me and live." Likewise, Jeremiah 29:12-13 says, "You will seek me and find me when you seek me with all your heart" (cf. Isa. 55:6-7). This same concept of wholeheartedness is idiomatic for the writer of Chronicles as well. He urges individuals "to give [their] heart to seek the Lord" (1 Chron. 22:19; 2 Chron. 11:16; or with "face" instead of "heart" in 2 Chron. 20:13). Another construction is "to set, establish one's heart to seek the Lord" (2 Chron. 19:3; cf. 12:14; 30:19). There can be no halfhearted relationship or search for God. Neither can one's repentance be halfhearted. We must enter into this commitment "with all our heart and with all our soul" (2 Chron. 15:12, 13, 15).

Seeking God involves: (1) voluntarily and wholeheartedly turning to God, (2) an inner attitude of devotion to serve Him, (3) a decision to turn away from all evil, (4) a decision to fulfill His will, and (5) a commitment to go to Him in fervent prayer. Furthermore, it is the chief means of averting evil (Amos 5:4, 14), the evidence of true humility (Zeph. 2:3), and the basis for sensing the presence of God (Hos. 5:15). All true repentance, communion with God, service for Him, prayer to Him, and spiritual growth in Him revolves around truly seeking the Lord.

When Asa tore down the pagan installations, smashed the sacred stones, and cut down the sacred groves of an Asherah, he not only demonstrated how sincere his search for God was, but he also acted on the basis and in the spirit of the Word of God commanded in Deuteronomy 7:5; 12:3; and 16:21-22. He also demonstrated what Proverbs 14:34 says: "Righteousness exalts a nation, but sin is a reproach to any people." Indeed, that is what Jeremiah put into alternative prospects for judgment or blessing on any nation in 18:7-10.

---

3. *Theological Dictionary of the Old Testament*, s.v. "Darash."

When the nation Israel sought the Lord, He gave them rest from all their enemies: "The land is still ours because we have sought the Lord our God" (2 Chron. 14:7). The connection is not accidental, nor is it meant merely as a casual comment. It is theology in its most real and practical form. It is both amusing and sad to see the mania of modern nations. They maintain a high state of military readiness but usually neglect the preparations of the hearts of their people to meet the high standards of the government of heaven. Of what use is the most sophisticated or unique weapons system on the face of the earth if that nation has flaunted righteousness, justice, and mercy or failed to walk humbly with the one true God?

For those who truly seek God, there is a second result that will follow.

## WE WILL EXPERIENCE GOD'S PRESENCE AGAIN (15:1-7)

Once again God used a prophet to stir up the hearts and consciences of the people and king. This time He sent Azariah, who spoke as the "Spirit of God came upon [him]" (v. 1). Azariah's challenge was, "The Lord is with you when you are with Him. If you seek Him, He will be found by you, but if you forsake Him, He will forsake you" (v. 2). Every other ambition, feeling, longing, and urge has to be set aside in favor of searching for the living God if we have any hopes of being found by Him.

The presence of God was not to be regarded lightly. Even though the king had just returned flushed with unbelievably great success on the battle field, he must not be any more presumptuous than we ought to be when the goodness of God deals with us more gently than we have a right to expect.

The text urges us to come into a deeper knowledge and fellowship with the living God. The Lord has been with us on many an occasion when we deserved it far less than Asa, in whose heart God had begun a reformation prior to a revival. Is it not time that we sought Him out with a new sense of hunger and thirst for righteousness? Oh, to know the joy, quietness, confidence, nourishment, and power of the abiding presence of the living God.

Azariah did not cater or pander to the ego of the monarch. He did not congratulate him on a splendid victory, nor did he try to worm his way into the higher echelons of government by indulging in unnecessary flattery over the crushing defeat of the Ethiopian king. Instead his message was one of going on in spiritual growth.

We are never so vulnerable as when we have had unusual success, for our heads are in danger of being turned by the headiness and extravagant praise such situations sometimes bring. Then more than ever we are in special need of being reminded that it is time we sought the Lord. His very goodness should lead us to a new sense of repentance and a deeper quest for the presence of God in our lives.

The informing theology of this truth may be found as far back as the word Moses delivered in Deuteronomy 4:29: "If from [the exile] you seek the Lord your God, you will find Him if you seek for Him with all your heart and with all your soul." This principle is now reinforced by a review of history in verses 3-6 of 2 Chronicles 15. It is amazing that there is no main verb in verse 3, thus three periods could be intended here: *the archaic past* in the experience of the judges of Israel, *the present condition* of the kingdom, and *the future* under the Assyrians, Babylonians, Greeks, or Romans. Apparently the writer was being deliberately ambiguous so his statement could be principlized. That is, its truth fits all times in a type of generic wholeness that embraces the common condition of all men apart from the presence of the Lord.

The price of our godlessness is as high today as it was yesterday for Israel; they were "without the true God" (v. 3). All attempts to live life apart from God leads to atheism, either real or practical. Acting as if God does not matter in some areas of life or as if we can handle things on our own until we get into trouble is to live without the true God. "But the Lord is the true God; He is the living God, the eternal King" (Jer. 10:10). The accent in this clause is on the predicate "true," for there is no truth apart from the author and maintainer of truth in all its forms.

A second price is in the absence of a teaching priest (v. 3). The priests in the Old Testament functioned as the community's teachers (Lev. 10:10; Deut. 33:10). But this is a most dangerous situation as well, for "where there is no vision [revelation or proclamation of that word], the people break loose [cast off all restraint and become ungovernable]" (Prov. 29:18; cf. Ex. 32:6).

And thirdly they were "without the law" (v. 3). How then shall we live? If there is no path to walk in, how shall we judge by what standard we are to make ethical, moral, or practical decisions? The psalmist was especially glad for the help the law of God gave him. It was more to be desired than honey and the honeycomb (Ps. 19:7-11).

Tragically, these three indictments summarize our day and the experience of all too many believers. The great human need, both past and present, is to "turn" (v. 4) and repent, for whenever people turned in the past, God was found by them. Without revival, our cities and streets will remain unsafe for travel, one nation will unjustly rise up against another (vv. 5-6), and one crisis after another will be precipitated: economic, domestic, international. Herein lies something more basic and necessary than the Geneva talks on disarmament. We have failed to seek God's solution. By not taking the gospel into the city, it has come to pass that we cannot even take our cars there, for fear that they will be stolen or vandalized.

The price for refusing to be renewed by the Spirit of God is very high. The nations themselves shall be put into a confusion (v. 6) as our Lord allows one nation to discipline another. Thus nations rise and fall according to the signal given from God.

Asa was instructed not to give up. He was to "be strong . . . for [his] work would be rewarded" (v. 7). The admonition is reminiscent of those given to Joshua, and the plea "do not give up" would be reflected later in Zephaniah 3:16, as would the promise about reward be reflected later in Jeremiah 31:16. It seems ridiculous for a man who had just had such a huge success to be challenged in this way. But his need is no more ludicrous than our own in similar circumstances. Often it is easier to face a hostile nation or army than it is to face evil and sin squarely. No doubt the writer of Chronicles uses the conscious exaggeration of hyperbole when he paints the picture of the past in such negative totalities in verses 5 and 6. But by putting it in such identifiable terms, readers through the centuries have recognized his formulation as having a great element of truth for describing their own circumstances and then for constructing their own view of the future.

In sum, we must "come near to God and He will draw near to [us]. [We] must wash [our] hands, [we] sinners, and purify [our] hearts, [we who are] double-minded" (James 4:8). This is one search we cannot afford to give up on.

There is one more result from our wholehearted search for God.

## WE WILL PREVAIL OVER OUR FOES (14:9-15; 16:1-10)

There are two examples to illustrate our point, one positive and one negative, unfortunately. When Asa depended on the Lord and sought Him with all his heart, his testimony was, "Lord, there is no one like you to help the powerless against the mighty" (14:11). The incomparability of God exceeds everything known to men or women. Asa's prayer in those early days was, "Help us O Lord our God, for we rely on you and in your name. . . . Do not let man prevail against you" (14:11). Even that word "rely" is important in this context (it also appears in 16:7 [twice] and 8). All other reliances are false and ultimately hopeless when compared to the God who exceeds everything we can think or imagine. So let us raise our own *Ebenezer* and mark it down well that no man or force can prevail against God or His people. He springs to the aid of those who themselves are powerless. And when it comes time to act, they act, think, and pray "in His name" (14:1). God will never abandon His people, church, or Word. But whether a nation or a denominational group will continue to experience that favor may be a different sort of question. The name of God will never lack for devotees or successful representatives to carry it around the world. On the other hand, God is not stuck with America, evangelicalism, or our special methodologies. He could raise up from Russia or China a whole new cadre of men and women who would rely on Him implicitly. No, it is not His cause that hangs in the balance; instead, it is we who are being weighed and found wanting if we do not turn to seek Him with all our hearts.

The Ethiopian army of Zerah was crushed before the army of Asa. The victory, as it always does under these sorts of circumstance, belonged to the Lord (vv. 13-14). As in those real contests of life, we must anticipate in our spiritual warfare more evidence of the power, victory, and success of the Lord's cause and name. It is embarrassing to realize that for almost one and one-half millennia the church has made little or no impact on the Islamic world. The church once flourished in North Africa. And what shall we say about so many other "hidden peoples" that have not yet been reached with the gospel? If there is no one like our Lord, and if we only need to turn to Him, seek Him with our whole hearts, and rely on Him alone to help the helpless, then why do we remain where we are? With the apostle Paul we shout, "Therefore be steadfast, immovable, always abounding in the work of the Lord, for you know that your labor is not in vain" (1 Cor. 15:58).

I wish this were the end of the chapter, but unfortunately Asa's life has another segment. He forgot, as we all too quickly tend to forget, the lessons he had learned earlier in his career with the Zerah incident. Faced with an unprovoked attack from northern Israel, he decided to "rely on the king of Syria" (16:7) to put some pressure on Israel by attacking them on their northern border. The idea was that while they were thus occupied, Asa would be able to recoup his resources on Israel's southern border and build up the fortifications. But what often makes good logical sense is not always good theological sense, especially if it runs directly counter to God's Word. In appealing to Ben-hadad, king of Syria, Asa introduced a military conqueror over his own relatives in the ten tribes to the north. Furthermore, by purchasing this military favor, he also tacitly recognized that he was weaker than, and therefore politically in subjection to, the Syrian ruler.

But God sent another prophet named Hanani to roundly rebuke him for his false reliance on human powers in preference to the Lord. All such reliances spell disaster. This includes all of the self-help emphasis of our day and all sociological and psychological explanations that do not have a realistic view of guilt, sin, or God. It is lethal to lean on another nation, philosophy, or methodology as a substitute for the living God.

When Asa had relied on the Lord, chided the prophet Hanani, He delivered them into his hand. Why had he suddenly thought better of that? Did he not know that "the eyes of the Lord go back and forth throughout all the earth to show Himself strong on behalf of those whose hearts are fully committed to Him" (16:9)? The omniscient eye of God still searches for those who are completely given over to Him. In the hands of God, ordinary, weak individuals who trust in the Lord with all their heart and soul suddenly become God's choice instruments, and they do mighty exploits for the Savior because God shows Himself strong on behalf of those who rely on Him.

There were three marks in Asa's decline. First, he allied himself with the Syrian king, Ben-hadad. Next, he angrily threw the prophet Hanani into prison for rebuking him. Finally, he relied on physicians to get well rather than relying on God. This third sin will trouble some in our modern culture who, of course, see nothing incongruous with their testimony and seeking help from medical doctors. But we must be careful not to translate our contemporary conception of physicians back to the ancient world. The physicians of that day depended not on scientific procedures but on incantations and magical remedies. To turn to them was tantamount to turning away from God. Thus Asa "did do a very foolish thing" (16:9). No longer was his heart "fully committed to the Lord" (15:17), and therefore no longer could he or Judah rejoice (15:15). What a waste after so many years of wonderful reformation and then times of great revival. More than ever we ought to be warned that it is not the person who begins the race that should boast, but only the one who takes off the equipment after the contest. It is always proper to seek the Lord.

The past decade and a half have been unusually good years in America. They should have led us to seek God in a way we have never done before. How can we explain the unusual strength of the dollar against other currencies? How can we explain the sudden and dramatic drop in our own double-digit inflation while other countries around the world continue to have soaring rates, sometimes reaching as high as several hundred percentage points per year? Again, against the best prognostications of the experts, how can we, simultaneously with these other features, have a drop in unemployment figures? And why should our gross national product and interest rates be holding so well? Are all of these factors pure accident? Or are they due to the human sagacity of the current government administration? No, God is speaking to us through His kindness. The very goodness of God is leading us to repentance. There is also the moral minority, that remnant for whose sake the rest of us are being given further opportunities to seek the Lord.

As the deer pants for the water, let our souls pant for the living God. "Is this the generation of those that seek Him, that seek His face" (Ps. 24:6)? May Christ's church be revived and search for Him as never before. May we know a new communion with the King of kings and Lord of lords. May we know what it is to serve, obey, and know Him in an altogether unique way, for if we seek Him, He will be found by each one of us.

# 6

## It Is Time to Pray to the Lord:

---

### REVIVAL UNDER JEHOSHAPHAT
### 2 Chronicles 20

**S**ome individuals, who are basically well meaning and who strive to do what is right, are also very naive and easily misled. King Jehoshaphat fitted squarely into this category. For even though he was a pious and successful monarch, he nevertheless had to be repeatedly censured by God's holy prophets. Four of them rebuked and corrected him when he became entangled in ungodly alliances and relationships. Jehu, the son of Hanani, charged him with helping Ahab and those who hated the Lord (19:2). Eliezer, the son of Dodavahu, charged him with being unequally yoked in a shipping venture at Ezion Geber (20:36-37). Micaiah, son of Imlah, roundly rebuked him for joining with Ahab to venture against Ramoth Gilead (18:16). And the Levite Jahaziel encouraged him as he went out to battle against the eastern nations (20:14-17). But for all of Jehoshaphat's sins and weaknesses of character, he mastered the discipline of prayer. And few chapters in the Bible can better illustrate the effectiveness and power of prayer than 2 Chronicles 20.

If 2 Chronicles 7:14 serves as the paradigm for the whole book, as I have argued, then chapter 20 and the events narrated from the life of Jehoshaphat focus on an important component of all revivals: prayer. The preaching of the Word moves men and women to humble themselves under the mighty hand of God and to turn from their wicked ways and seek God's face in a renewed way. Prayer moves God to graciously pour out the blessing of heaven on sinners, undeserving as we are.

The writer of Chronicles clearly wanted to lift high the kingdom of Israel under David and Solomon as the model and the forerunner of the messianic kingdom. Although the latter kingdom was already realized in principle, from his perspective it was also still future in the two advents of Christ. Therefore all the successors on the Davidic throne were likewise subjects of great interest, for each was a transmitter of that ancient promise and the heart of its present manifestation. Accordingly, the role they play in worship, their responsiveness to the proclaimed Word of God, and the leadership they give to the things of God will be very determinative in the life of the people. Jehoshaphat was most instrumental in leading his people into a new experience of the power of God through prayer.

This is not the first time the Chronicler expressed an interest in prayer. He had inserted the brief plaintive cry of Jabez to God even in the midst of rehearsing the genealogies (1 Chron. 4:9-10; God's response was also recorded: "And God granted his request"). Then there was Solomon's prayer for wisdom (2 Chron. 1:8-11; 9:22), which God also granted most generously, Asa's prayer for deliverance in the midst of the crisis precipitated by Zerah the Ethiopian (2 Chron. 14:9-15), and Hezekiah's prayer for a lengthened life (2 Chron. 32:24-25). But the prayer that forms the best model for our praying is that of Jehoshaphat in 2 Chronicles 20.

This raises the question of what it means to pray. Briefly, when we pray we make our request known to God by the help of the Holy Spirit; in the name, authority, and mediation of our Lord Jesus Christ; with faith, fervency, and submission to the will of God; and with sole reference to His honor and glory. Each part of this rather elaborate definition is important and plays a role in our entering into prayer.

First, the efficient cause of prayer must be the Holy Spirit. James 5:16 translated literally teaches us that it is the "prayer worked in by the Holy Spirit that is effective." Thus all prayer that is not prompted by the Word of God or worked in, that is, energized by, the Holy Spirit is just so much howling in the ears of God. But if it be objected, as it surely will, that the Spirit of God was not present in the Old Testament or that He did not so function, then consider David's request in Psalm 51:11 that the Holy Spirit not be taken from him. Also note the rebuke that Jesus gave (prior to the cross) to Nicodemus for his ignorance of the ministry of the Holy Spirit in the process of regeneration (John 3); the Lord was horrified that Nicodemus could be a teacher and still not know about that ministry. So there is a strong case for the work of the Holy Spirit in the life of the believer in the Old Testament.

The only proper object of prayer is God. Thus the aim of our praying ought to be the glory and honor of His name, and our requests ought to be in accordance with His will. That is why many believers end their prayers with a statement like "all these things we ask in Jesus' name." This is not a magical password or a talisman. It says that we wish for nothing that is not in accordance with the high and holy will of the living God. "This is the confidence that we have in Him, that if we ask anything *according to His will*, He will hear us" (1 John 5:14).

Moreover, our prayers must be offered in faith, "nothing wavering" (James 1:6), and we must approach the throne of grace "believing that He is and He is a rewarder. . ." (Heb. 11:6). Also our prayers must be with fervency (James 5:16). There can be no prayers of incense offered up without any fire.

Prayer then is the great means the Father has opened up for making our requests known and for joining in the work of ministry around the world. Prayer is God's sovereign medicine and remedy for the afflicted mind. Being able to approach God is one of the inestimable privileges we have as believers, a gift won for us by the death of Christ.

But God already knows our wants and desires, so why pray? The answer is that we pray not so much to inform God as to draw our own affections towards Him and the holy things for which we plead. But is it not vain to pray, especially because our prayers cannot alter the providence of God? The answer is no. The same providence that orders the end orders the means by which that end is obtained, and part of that means is our prayer. Therefore, just as God has decreed the blessing, so He has decreed that the blessing should come by prayer. Hence prayer is not an optional, spiritual luxury; it is a must.

How then should we pray if we wish our prayers to be acceptable to God? Here are some suggestions. First, if we want God to hear us, we must begin by hearing Him (Prov. 1:24-28). Second, we must deeply desire what we ask for. "He who asks coldly, begs only a denial." Third, we must come with sufficient resolve to wait for the answer. Fourth, we must not pray for things that are purely selfish and only for our own gratification (James 4:3). Finally, we must stress praying for some grand purpose and avoid a narrow provincialism that sees only one's immediate household, friends, or church as the object of prayers. An example of a grand prayer that lifts us beyond narrow, myopic prayers is the one that focuses on the need for revival in our day.

2 Chronicles 20 gives us five *reasons* to pray, each of which adds fresh incentive to this most holy exercise of the soul. They are:

1. God rules over all kingdoms of the nations (v. 6).
2. God delights to do what He promised to do (vv. 7-11).
3. God judges all who oppose His work (v. 12).
4. God delivers us from all our distresses (vv. 14-17).
5. God upholds those who believe Him and His Word (vv. 18-30).

When King Jehoshaphat had been confronted with an army of huge proportions, he resolved to take the matter immediately to the Lord in prayer. In fact, he gathered the entire population of Judah, including the men, wives, and little ones (20:13). The people came from every town in Judah to seek the Lord's face (20:4). It was on this occasion that the king stood up and led them in this most instructive prayer. He begged God to intervene on their behalf, and in the process he gave these five reasons to pray.

## GOD RULES OVER ALL THE KINGDOMS OF THE NATIONS (20:6)

In the way he addressed God, we learn with what confidence Jehoshaphat came to the Lord in prayer. That confidence is instructive, teaching us that God is the God who has given His promise to the patriarchs Abraham, Isaac, and Jacob. He rules the world on the basis of this ancient but ever renewing plan, which He began to disclose shortly after the Fall. Furthermore, God's authority extends over all of heaven and earth. It is as Nebuchadnezzar learned by hard experience: "The most High is sovereign over the kingdoms of men and gives them to whomever He wishes and sets them over the lowliest of men" (Dan. 4:17, cf. 25). It is no wonder, then, that no one ever has or ever will successfully resist or block His will.

For this reason we must never regard prayer lightly. Among all the potentates and controllers of power-blocs in the world, none comes even close to equaling the Lord's authority, might, and ability to rectify things. Let us therefore come boldly as we approach His throne of grace for mercy and seasons of refreshing. Once He has been pleased to move in times of revival, who or what can withstand Him? May God grant us a new vision of His incomparable greatness. This is the best cure for our faintheartedness. If we have not because we have not asked, let us pray to the Lord, who owns and runs the universe. Down will come all the strongholds and deep pockets of resistance to the gospel when we storm the gates of heaven and pray that our Father would vanquish these heavily ensconced foes.

## GOD DELIGHTS TO DO WHAT HE PROMISED (20:7-11)

Founding our prayers on the promises of God is not meant to teach us to pray timidly, as though worried about asking for anything not explicitly written in the Scriptures. It is rather an important exercise in learning to pray in accordance with God's will. Furthermore, these promises were not given to excuse us from praying but to teach us what to pray for and how to pray for it.

The promises on which Jehoshaphat based his prayer dealt with the gift of the land to Israel forever (Gen. 13:15; 15:18). By extrapolation the situation of an unprovoked enemy attack fell within the boundaries of these promises and offered great grounds for the king to ask for their defeat (2 Chron. 20:7).

Also, at the dedication of the Temple, the Lord had promised Solomon that He would hear the prayers of His people, whether Jewish or Gentile (2 Chron. 6:14-42; 7:15). He said: "My eyes will be open, and my ears attentive to the prayers offered in this place."

The Lord expects us to obey Him as Abraham did and thus was called the "friend of God" (v. 7; James 2:23). Indeed, "[we] are [His] friends if [we] do whatsoever [He] commands [us]" (John 15:14).

Furthermore, when we are in distress—and God anticipated we would be at times—we should take that to Him in prayer. This was anticipated in Solomon's request in 2 Chronicles 6:28-30 referred to by Jehoshaphat (20:9). Jeremiah also said it well: "You shall seek me and find me, when you shall search for me with all your heart" (Jer. 29:13). This latter verse was used in the life of a young lawyer who was studying for the bar. But God had other plans for him, and Charles G. Finney was soundly converted and called into a ministry of evangelism and revivals. According to his own testimony, God used this verse as one of the most significant challenges in his own life.

The promise of God is that He will hear and be found by all those who search for Him with all their hearts. Now that has to be one of the greatest inducements that has ever been given to a ministry of prayer. As Luke's gospel puts it, "if [we] being evil know how to give good gifts to [our] children; how much more shall [our] heavenly Father give the Holy Spirit to those [of us] who ask Him?" (Luke 11:13). Why do we not ask?

## GOD JUDGES ALL WHO OPPOSE HIS WORK (20:12)

In many ways the word *judge* epitomized the message of Jehoshaphat, whose name means "Yahweh will judge." But it is also a recognition of our own impotence: God must judge, not we. Asa realized that he, too, was powerless in this situation (2 Chron. 14:11), but God delivered him because he relied on the name of the Lord. Thus when we, like Jehoshaphat, "do not know what to do" (v. 12), we should do what he did and turn "our eyes upon [Him]" (v. 12).

Wisdom has been promised to those who lack it, and this text is another example of such. The psalmist testified, "My eyes are ever on the Lord, for only He will release my feet from the snare" (Ps. 25:15), and, "As the eyes of slaves look to their master, and the eyes of the maid to her mistress, so our eyes look to the Lord our God until He shows us His mercy" (Ps. 123:2). Finally, he said, "But my eyes are fixed on you, O Lord of Hosts; in you I take refuge. Do not give me over to death" (Ps. 141:8).

There is no need to keep score or to worry if might will make right in a world where God is the final and only real judge. Though we may be buffeted by enigmas and distresses, we can fly to our Lord in prayer and seek His help. Surely He knows how to right the wrongs and to silence the unprovoked attacks. He is the supreme judge of all the earth.

## GOD DELIVERS US FROM OUR DISTRESSES (20:14-17)

In this paragraph we are introduced to another specially prepared individual who was enabled by the Holy Spirit to do what God wanted him to do in ministering to Jehoshaphat. His name was Jahaziel the son of Zechariah. This Levitical singer and fifth generation ancestor of Mattaniah (perhaps the same Mattaniah who was the son of Asaph, mentioned in 1 Chron. 25:2, 12) was just as much filled with the Holy Spirit as the New Testament apostles.

Through him the Lord answered Jehoshaphat's prayer of distress. His main word, which is repeated twice and is therefore an *inclusio,* or frame, for his message, is "Do not be afraid" (vv. 15, 17). How many times does the Lord need to remind us that we must forgo our phobias? Repeatedly the Bible urges us to "fear not" and then usually quickly adds "for I am with you." And that is the promise attached to the prohibition here (v. 17).

The encouraging word was, "The battle is not yours, but God's" (v. 15). Thus the theology was the same as that of 1 Samuel 17:47 in the David and Goliath situation: "All those gathered here will know that it is not by sword or spear that the Lord saves; for the battle is the Lord's and He will give all of you into our hands." Later on, Nehemiah would comfort his badly shaken workers by saying, "Don't be afraid. . . . Remember the Lord who is great and awesome" (Neh. 4:14). In his case, too, the battle was to be most unusual, for Israel would not be required to fight at all, because the Lord would fight for them.

There were things to do, however. The Israelites were to "take [their] place, stand still, and watch the salvation of the Lord" (v. 17). The command was reminiscent of the one given to Moses at the Red Sea, when Pharaoh's army was closing in and Israel was trapped by the mountains, the sea, and the enemy; every word is the same except for the additional phrase "stand still" (Ex. 14:13). This was one of those occasions when all frantic human activity was to be of no avail. It was time to trade business for worship.

To those who come to God in earnest prayer, He will grant deliverance regardless of the odds. How slow we are to capitalize on this fact of spiritual life. Too frequently we assume that deliverance rests in our hands. But just one moment of serious reflection should tell us that such is not the case. Nor was it so on this occasion, for God worked mightily on Israel's behalf.

If only we would learn how to be strong and not be afraid. If only we would realize what a difference the presence of God makes in every testing or opportunity of life. Haggai reminded the people of his day of this fact (Hag. 2:4-5). Indeed, the little preposition *with* appears over a hundred times in conjunction with the promise of the real, powerful, comforting presence of the living God.

## GOD UPHOLDS THOSE WHO HAVE FAITH IN HIM AND HIS WORD (20:18-30)

Jehoshaphat's response to Jahaziel's ministry of the word of God was to lead the people in bowing their heads and falling down in worship. And then, surprisingly, some of the Levites stood up and broke out in praise. The revival was on. How God's people love to praise Him when their burdens have been lifted. How spontaneous is the gift of doxology and music when our guilt, concerns, and sins have been cast on the burden bearer. Verses 18-19 are among those select passages of Scripture in the Old Testament that show us that every great once in a while God's people can and do respond beautifully to the call of the Word of God. And how wonderful it is when this happens. May our own hearts long to own up to a similar confession, and may the joy of our lives be the high honor of raising our voices in the praise and magnification of the God of gods and Lord of lords.

Early the next morning the king addressed the people with a summons to a new display of faith in the Lord. In fact, he used a play on the same words that the Holy Spirit used later when speaking through the prophet Isaiah to King Ahaz in the very famous virgin birth passage (Isa. 7:9). The king said, in a wonderful pun, "Have faith in the Lord your God and you will have staith" (2 Chron. 20:20). The Hebrew term translated "faith" and "staith" is the word we have anglicized into "amen." Thus he urged, to put it in other words that attempt to capture the pun in English, "Be sure in the Lord you will be secure," or, "Affirm the Lord and you will be confirmed," or, "Stand firm in your Lord and you will be stood firm."

How cowardly we act when we put our trust in ourselves, our institutions, money, growth, political pull, intellectual analysis, or our own resourcefulness, rather than putting our trust in the Lord. It was Isaiah who announced this principle best: "You will keep that person in perfect peace whose mind is stayed on [the Lord], because he trusts in [the Lord]" (Isa. 26:3). Also he added, "The one who trusts [in the Lord] will never be dismayed" (Isa. 28:16). We ask in surprise, "What, *never* be dismayed?" No, we will never be dismayed when our hearts are garrisoned about by their trust in the living God.

In verse 20b Jehoshaphat commended the word of the prophets to our trust as well, for we must trust the Word of God just as much as we trust the Lord. For how will we ever know how to live or think if we do not have the Word from His holy prophets and apostles? Indeed, without such a faith in the Word of God, we shall be denied every opportunity for success and for a genuine revival in our day. Our cry must be, "Back to the Book, the Word and the testimonies of our Lord." More than anything else, we need an end to the awful famine of the Word of God in our day. Too frequently we have settled for talking *about* the Word of God without a patient listening to it, the whole context, the whole counsel of God from Genesis to Revelation proceeding line after line, verse after verse, and paragraph after paragraph. This can only lead to spiritual malnutrition and as Amos described it, "a famine of hearing the words of the Lord" (Amos 8:11).

Much of the blame for this state of affairs must lie at the doorstep of the ministry—not all ministers, mind you, but all too many in our day. We must painfully reflect on this phenomenon. In the words of Charles G. Finney,

> And ministers ought to know that nothing is more common than for spiritual Christians to feel burdened and distressed at the state of the ministry. I would not wake up any wrong feelings towards ministers, but it is time . . . that their souls are kindled up. . . . When a minister has gone as far as his experience in spiritual exercises goes, there he stops; and until he has a renewed experience . . . [and] his heart is broken afresh . . . he will help them no more.
>
> He may preach sound doctrine . . . but, after all, his preaching will want that searching pungency, that practical bearing, that unction. . . . However much intellectual furniture [he] may possess, [he remains] in a state of *spiritual babyhood*. . . . [He] needs to be fed [rather] than to undertake to feed the Church of God.[1]

When both of these objects of trust were understood and held in proper balance, the people broke out into song. Thus singing was not restricted to the Temple but was just as at home amid the dangers of life as it was in the quiet sanctuary of God. Like Paul and Silas, who sang at midnight in prison at Philippi (Acts 16:25), the Israelites sang when faced by evil forces.

The praise of God is directed towards the beauty of His holiness (v. 21). The phrase probably refers to the summation of all God's attributes and the dazzling array that His person cast on the scene where He was present. The invitation to worship God in the beauty of holiness is frequently given (e.g., 1 Chron. 16:29; Ps. 96:9; and in part in Ps. 29:2 and 110:3). Accordingly, the phrase also involves the element of the spiritual character of God's people as they come to worship Him. Our outward and inward attire is not an inconsequential matter when it comes to appearing before the living God.

In most of the revivals known to us from Scripture, there is the thrill of the great joy that accompanies the genuine revival of God's people. Verse 27 tells us why: "The Lord had given them cause to

---

1. Charles G. Finney, *Revivals on Religion* (Westwood, N. J.: Revell, n.d.), pp. 126-27.

rejoice." Moreover, a holy terror and fear that originates from God overtakes the hearts of those who raise their fists against the living God (v. 29). But the peace of God is reserved for all who trust in Him. Thus verse 30 says that "God had given him rest on every side."

So concludes another example of a great Old Testament revival. Rather than stressing the doctrine of prayer by repeating the word over and over as in the revival of Asa (and as in the next two revivals in 2 Chronicles), the chronicler demonstrated the effectiveness and necessity of prayer by illustrating how effective it was in the life of King Jehoshaphat and his times.

If prayer carried the day for these people, then we ought to learn to make our appeal to heaven as well. There is no higher court of appeal or avenue of influence among mortals. Let us therefore let our prayers begin to flow to heaven. May they find their authority in our Lord's promises, and may they find their poignancy in our current needs for cleansing and genuine revival.

Prayer must be the hallmark of our Christian lives and the ministry of the church. It must become our number one priority if we are ever going to be more than a minority band exercising selective holding actions until the Lord returns. Such minimalistic goals are a weariness to God and a bother to mankind in general.

One more observation: our prayers must enlarge in their scope. All too frequently we ask only for ourselves and for our immediate environment. Where are the worldwide concerns that our Lord taught us to have? Where is the passion for the success of the Lord's cause around the face of the globe and in every people-group known? As Charles G. Finney observed:

> A backslidden heart . . . reveal[s] itself in praying almost exclusively for *self* . . . or friends. . . . It is often very striking and even shocking to attend a backslider's prayer meeting. . . . Their prayers are timid and hesitating and reveal the fact that they have little or no faith.[2]

Is it not time that we began to pray and to pray in the biblical manner? And has this passage not taught us why we ought to pray? May our God mercifully lead His church once again into a ministry of prayer.

---

2. Ibid., p. 498.

# 7

# It Is Time to Turn Back to the Lord:

## REVIVAL UNDER HEZEKIAH
## 2 Chronicles 30:1-9

Ernest Baker, in his pioneering study of Old Testament revivals, began his remarks on the revival under Hezekiah with this arresting assessment: "The revival in the time of Hezekiah is amongst the most sudden of those recorded in Scripture. Hezekiah began a work of reformation during the first month of his reign, and within two months the whole land was swept with a wave of spiritual enthusiasm."[1] It is not always possible for us to say why there is such a sudden response as the one under Hezekiah. Surely it is finally due only to the Spirit of God's moving on the hearts of men and women. But what secondary causes, if any, were present and specially used by the Spirit of God in this situation are not directly stated.

One factor can clearly be ruled out, and that is any positive influence that may have come from Hezekiah's father, Ahaz. On the contrary, the period under Ahaz, king of Judah, was the epitome of evil. For the sixteen years just preceding the revival he had done little more than poison the spiritual life of the people (2 Chron. 28:1-27). Everything Ahaz did led the people further away from God. The chronicle of his deeds reads like a litany of woes, for each act was another nail in his coffin and contribution to the spiritual doldrums of the nation. To

1. Ernest Baker, *The Revivals of the Bible* (Capetown, South Africa: Miller, 1906), p. 66.

mention a few, we note first of all that he "cast idols for worshiping Baals" (2 Chron. 28:2), mixing the worship of the various Baal idols with his worship of Molech (v. 3). To this he added the burning of incense in the Valley of Hinnom and on the hills and under every spreading tree (vv. 3, 4). But worst of all, he also burned his children as a sacrifice to the god Molech (v. 3).

Such unspeakable carnality, sensuality, and cruelty is reprehensible enough in the eyes of good and decent men. Imagine its effect on the living God. The unbridled licentiousness that accompanied much of the Canaanite worship of Baal and his consorts is well documented from the oldest discovered alphabetic script in the world, the Ugaritic documents found at modern Ras Shamra in Syria. My doctoral dissertation was on the Ugaritic pantheon, and I can testify that modern pornography seldom exceeds the debauchery to which these gods and goddesses and their devotees gave themselves. It is no wonder that the next statement that follows in verse 5 reads, "Wherefore the Lord his God handed him over to the king of Syria."

Do not miss the point here, for this is no odd instance from a bygone day with which we have nothing, or very little, in common. We, too, can be caught up in sensuality. In fact, the modern entertainment industry by and large panders to our thirst for, indeed, our adoration of, sensuality. Many theaters, night clubs, movies, and television programs go straight for the fleshly heart when they glorify lewdness, indecency, and immorality and generally flaunt every law of God. Such foul corrupters of the spiritual life are every bit as effective as the ancient worship of Baal and Molech in distracting hearts and minds from that which is pure, holy, beautiful, and true.

Even the abominable practice of offering live babies to Molech by placing them on the arms of the hollow-bellied furnaces that served as replicas of the alleged deity has its modern counterpart. Then the priestly drums rolled and the clamor of song and the noise of music ascended to heaven as these little ones rolled gently down the arms of idolatrous monstrosities and into their brimstone bellies for an offering to Molech. But how much different is the same act repeated in the sterilized environment of an abortion clinic or a hospital today? If we continue to destroy one and one-half million babies a year by abortion, will not God also hand us over into the hands of our enemy? Our greatest threat is not the Soviet Union or any other nation; our greatest threat is ourselves. If we do not soon repent and turn back to God, we are going to face some of the most difficult times we have ever faced as a nation.

Verse 19 of 2 Chronicles 28 is startling. It says that the Lord "humbled Judah because of Ahaz, . . . for he *cast off all restraint* in Judah and he was most unfaithful to the Lord." The remarkable fact about the words in italics is that they translate the same verb that was used to describe the enormity of Israel's sin in the golden calf incident (Ex. 32:25). It is the verb meaning "to make naked," "to let the reins loose," or "to become unbridled, lawless, or ungovernable." Wilbur Smith once asked,

> Can you think of any single phrase of four words [*cast off all restraint*] which would more perfectly describe our modern civilization than these? It seems as though economically, socially, domestically, in the home, in business, in the nation, throughout the world, men have thrown aside all restraint, and live, and act, and think, and plan, as though there were no universal law of recompense, as though men would never be punished for breaking the law of God, as though the future would take care of itself, and as though we should live only for the immediate present.[2]

As a result, Judah was plagued with a host of problems. Such wickedness cannot go unbridled without the love of God suddenly calling that people to justice. Wherefore, there came a period of severe military weakness. A number of the people were carried away captive to Syria (v. 5). Moreover, the northern kingdom inflicted a devastating defeat on Judah, carting off in naked disgrace upwards of two hundred thousand women, sons, and daughters, as was the habit in that day (v. 8). Other nations repeated the same feat, for Ahaz also had trouble from the Philistines and the Edomites. But rather than call on God for help, he appealed to the king of Assyria. Instead of the expected help, however, he was further insulted and robbed by the king he had hoped would be his ally (vv. 16-21).

For most of us this would have been enough trouble to force us in humility to a confession of our sin, but not Ahaz. "He became even more unfaithful to the Lord" (v. 22). He now sacrificed also to the gods of Syria (v. 23), the very nation that had defeated him. If these gods had helped Syria, he reasoned, then he would fall down to them, and perhaps they would help him also (v. 23). It is tragic to see how sin corrupts the reasoning powers, common sense, and wisdom of those who refuse to turn back to God but who instead continue on their reckless path of destruction. The chronicler curtly concluded, "But

2. Wilbur M. Smith, *The Glorious Revival Under King Hezekiah* (Grand Rapids: Zondervan, 1937), p. 12.

[the gods of Damascus] were for his ruin and for the downfall of all Israel" (v. 23).

From this point on Ahaz's evil knew no sane boundaries. He "shut the doors of the Lord's Temple" and took all the furniture and implements from the Temple and cut them up (v. 24). He built altars for pagan worship in every town in Judah (v. 25). His wickedness was so extravagant there was no hope of anything but more evil. The time was long overdue for the nation and its leadership to turn to God. And this was the ministry that God gave to the young son of Ahaz.

How did this evil man produce such a godly son as Hezekiah? Surely the fact that he did is one of the best refutations of the oft repeated but badly understood warning that the sins of the fathers visit the children to the third and fourth generation. That is only true when the children agree in the evil of their fathers and decide to walk in their footsteps. However, in this case Hezekiah saw the wickedness of his father and refused outright to imitate it, and God blessed him. He could not beg off having any responsibility for his situation by using the excuse of those to whom Jeremiah and Ezekiel later prophesied. Those rebels said in effect, "The 'old man' has sinned, and therefore there is no use fighting city hall" (Jer. 31:29; Ezek. 18:2). Even in those days, however, these two prophets had to protest vigorously that "the soul that sins, it is that soul or individual that shall die" (Ezek. 18:4).

Hezekiah is a man who began to practice what he preached before he commended it to others. Without any immediate influences for good that we can detect from a human point of view, Hezekiah opened the closed doors of the Temple and inaugurated services of worship and sacrifice once again. His words were bluntly to the point: "Our fathers were unfaithful; they did evil in the eyes of the Lord our God and forsook him. They turned their faces away from the Lord's dwelling place and turned their backs on him. . . . Therefore, the anger of God has fallen on Judah and Jerusalem. . . . This is why our fathers have fallen by the sword. . . . Now I intend to make a covenant with the Lord, the God of Israel, so that his fierce anger will turn away from us. My sons, do not be negligent now" (2 Chron. 29:6-11, NIV).

But a revival does not only depend on the open doors of the house of worship or on the existence of divine services. More is needed than these outward acts of piety. There must be a turning around. That turning is twofold: it is a turning *from* sin, the first ninety degree turn, and a turning *towards* God, the second ninety degree turn, to make a complete about-face.

The informing theology of Hezekiah's revival can be found in that great parting word of Moses, uttered just before he passes on to glory in Deuteronomy 30. Three times (vv. 2, 8, 10) Moses there urges Israel to return to the Lord if ever they are tempted to wander away from Him.

The Hebrew word "to turn or repent" is pronounced *shuv*. And in every one of the 118 instances where the word occurs with a religious significance, God was trying to give His people a *shove* in the right direction. The earliest prophetic use of *shûb* is found in the revival that took place under Samuel (1 Sam. 7:3). All the prophets, both in word and deed, referred to it and to the activity of repentance as the quintessence of their ministry. Therefore, it is probably the one expression that summarizes the whole prophetic ministry. In Zechariah 1:4, Zechariah, the next to the last prophet, chides, "All the earlier prophets proclaimed, 'This is what the Lord of Hosts says, "Turn from your evil ways and your evil deeds."'" Likewise 2 Kings 17:13 agrees: "The Lord warned Israel and Judah through all His prophets and seers: 'Turn from your evil ways.'" Accordingly, the word appears ten times in Isaiah, twenty-eight times in Jeremiah, twenty times in Ezekiel, seven times in Hosea, five times in Amos, and three each in Zechariah and Malachi.

The word appears thirteen times in 2 Chronicles (6:24, 26, 37, 38; 7:14, 19; 15:4; 30:6, 8, 9; 36:13) but five times in 2 Chronicles 30:6-9. This is probably due to the influence of 2 Chronicles 7:14, and therefore its use in chapter 30 reflects a thematic declaration. Thus, the keynote for this passage is the doctrine of repentance.

In this short selection from the four chapters dealing with the marvelous years of this monarch's reign there are four *alternatives*. Each one is a call to turn from wickedness and sin, as that programmatic verse of 2 Chronicles 7:14 had specified. The four *alternatives* are:

1. Turn to Him with an unqualified trust, or He will not turn to us (v. 6).
2. Turn to Him with a wholehearted obedience, or He will make us despicable to all (v. 7).
3. Turn to Him with glad service, or He will not turn His anger from us (v. 8).
4. Turn to Him with unceasing prayer, or He will withdraw His presence and favor from us (v. 9).

And just as Hezekiah announced under the inspiration of the Holy

Spirit some seven centuries before the first advent of Christ, it is time again to turn to the Lord. We, like those Judahites of old, must turn from our sin and turn to God if we wish to enjoy the fullness of the new life in Christ. Therefore, we are faced with the same four alternatives that Hezekiah set forth to the people of his day in the letter he sent by couriers throughout Israel and Judah (30:6).

### TURN TO HIM WITH AN UNQUALIFIED TRUST OR HE WILL NOT TURN TO US (30:6)

Turning to Yahweh demands an unqualified and unconditional trust in Him and an equivalent renunciation of every other coalition, secret love, or means of support. The totality of this commitment is the central issue. As Jeremiah evaluated the situation, he concluded, "We are here: we come to thee, for thou, Lord, art God. Valueless, indeed, is the idolatrous commotion on the mountains; truly in the Lord, our God, is the help/salvation of Israel" (Jer. 3:22b-23). The fact that there is no one else to turn to beside the Lord is the point also made by Hosea: "Assur cannot save us; we will not ride upon horses; neither will we say anymore to the work of our hands, you are our gods; for in you the righteous find mercy" (Hos. 14:4)

The fact that we are being bidden to return to the Lord implies that we are in a backslid state. At first all of us will attempt to deny this strong assertion or implication. Like the men and women of Malachi's day, we will retort, "Who, us? We are to return?" (Mal. 3:7). But backsliding is one of our key diseases. It consists of taking back our consecration to the Lord, leaving our first love for God, abstaining from the regular and wholehearted devotion to God in worship and prayer, and maintaining the outward forms of religion without the realities. Briefly stated, "The backslider in heart is filled with his or her own ways" (Prov. 14:14). Thus, like the church at Ephesus, many of us "have left [our] first love" (Rev. 2:4). If some of us believe that the message to repent is misdirected when it is aimed at the church, we need only to examine the opening of the book of Revelation a little closer. There the apostle John called four of the seven churches to which he wrote to repent (Rev. 2:5, 16, 21; 3:3).

As has been mentioned already, there are two aspects of repentance. Forty-eight of the 118 religious uses of the word (which incidentally is found altogether some 1,056 times) appear with the preposition "to" or "unto" and usually with the Lord as the object. That is the positive aspect of repentance. But it must be preceded by a negative aspect in which we "turn from" evil and sin. Consequently, "turn" or "repent" appears forty times with the preposition "from." Both actions are needed. In fact, turning, or conversion as it is known from the Latin root word, is the whole process whereby we turn from sin and to the Lord. The first action, which involves godly sorrow for sin, is called repentance, and the second action, which reaches out to receive what God has given to us, is called faith. That is how we come to faith in Christ, and that is how we continue to live by faith as well.

The promise that God would hear His children when they come to their senses in their state of backsliding is as old as Moses. He advised: "When you are in trouble and all these words come to pass in the last days, then you will *turn back* to the Lord your God and listen to His voice. For the Lord your God is a merciful God. He will not abandon or destroy you and He will not forget the covenant, which He promised by oath to your fathers" (Deut. 4:30-31). And that is the same promise-plan in which we are still sharing.

The object of our affections must be none other than the God of Abraham, Isaac, and Jacob. The incomparably great God is the base of all true religion, and the promise-plan is the central plan by which the Lord has been operating the universe since the experience in Eden. But when our hearts are sold out to other coalitions, loves, and priorities, then we are entrapped by our own sin. As Hosea said, "Their deeds do not permit them to return to their God. A spirit of prostitution is in their heart; they do not acknowledge the Lord" (Hos. 5:4).

The alternative of 2 Chronicles 30:6 is this: "Return to the Lord . . . so that He may return to you." How else can we experience once again the full power and presence of the living Lord? One of the saddest texts in Scripture is Hosea 5:15: "I will go to my place *until* they admit their guilt and seek my face and in their misery they earnestly seek me." Consequently, instead of enjoying the Lord's countenance as requested in the Aaronic benediction of Numbers 6:24-26, we feel separated, powerless, ashamed, bored, and let down. But if we turn from our wicked ways, we will once again sense that God is gracious, making His face to shine on us and giving us peace.

The great hope of Scripture, and of our Lord, is that "perhaps [we] will listen and each [of us] will turn from [our] wicked way. Then [He] will relent and not bring on [us] the disaster [He] was planning" (Jer. 26:3). We must make the first move if God is to normalize relations between us and we are to have His favor turned full force on us again.

O let us turn for His name's sake and for our own good.

### TURN TO HIM WITH A WHOLEHEARTED OBEDIENCE OR HE WILL MAKE US DESPICABLE TO ALL (30:7)

We are likewise urged to turn from our deadening obsession with failures of the past. Too frequently we assume that we are heirs of an irreversible situation, and thus we are excused for not taking any direct or personal action to turn around. But this defeatist's mentality only falls into its own trap. It insists on following the sins of the fathers or in saying that since the fathers have sinned, what can we do? But Hezekiah avoided that trap. Few have ever had as godless an example to follow, and yet few have excelled as well as he. He refused to settle for the performance level of the past or present generation. And we must come out from hiding behind our contemporaries.

Of course that generation was sinful, and of course we may be no worse than they were. But the grace of God will not always tarry, and we cannot presume upon His patience forever. It is high time we acted. Each generation and every individual in it must answer to God. The alternative is the horrifying prospect of national disgrace. Unfaithfulness ultimately has a very high price, even for a secular culture. If we continue in it, we will then slide from the dizzying heights of being regarded as the most favored among the nations to the status of utter contempt.

There are those who feel that we began to experience some of this in the 1960s. It became popular then to take potshots at United States citizens abroad, calling them "ugly Americans," for instance. The vice president was pelted with rotten fruit, eggs, and verbal abuse. Even those nations that had received millions of dollars in aid from this country or those whose distress we responded to when they were surrounded by enemies joined merrily in the new game of denouncing the "imperialistic" Americans. What is certain, however, is that if we continue to turn our backs on God, He will turn His back on us and make us despicable among the nations.

The word "unfaithfulness" and its associated terms appear frequently in Chronicles and always in passages that have no parallel in the books of Samuel or Kings. As it is used by the chronicler, unfaithfulness is evidenced by worship of pagan deities, lack of purity in the heart, and lack of obedience to the Word of the Lord. Hezekiah's father, Ahaz, we have seen, promoted wickedness (2 Chron. 28:19), and "in his time of trouble . . . he became even more unfaithful to the Lord" (28:22).

Such unfaithfulness regularly invited punishment, usually military defeat or exile and the like. Israel had been taught this harsh lesson as early as the reign of its first king, Saul. But modern nations must not think that the ground rules have changed or that God has eased up on His requirements for fellowship and favor. The truth of the matter is that we, if anything, are more vulnerable today than ever before, because we have so much more knowledge and have been exposed to so much more of the favor and graciousness of the plan and salvation of God. Where grace abounds, so does responsibility.

## Turn to Him with Glad Service
## or He Will Not Turn His Anger from Us (30:8)

Three commands are given to those who are willing to turn: "submit to the Lord," "come to the sanctuary," and "serve the Lord your God" (v. 8). By observing these injunctions we shall avoid being "stiff-necked," as the previous generations were.

To submit is literally "to give the hand to the Lord." This same expression found in verse 8 is used in 1 Chronicles 29:24, "[All the leaders] pledged their submission to [literally, "gave the hand under"] Solomon the king." Thus the hand is given (i.e., raised) as a pledge of fidelity (cf. 1 Kings 10:15; Ezra 10:19; Ezek. 17:18). The condition of being stiff-necked, on the other hand, is a permanent condition of the unregenerate, who resist the Holy Spirit (Acts 7:15). How could believers remain permanently poised against their Lord? Let us therefore raise our hands in pledge of our loyalty and fidelity to God and serve in full submission under His lordship.

We must also come to His sanctuary, for it is impossible to turn to God without also turning to the place where we corporately meet Him. God has consecrated the sanctuary concept in both Testaments, and we only defraud ourselves when we forsake the assembling of ourselves together, as the habit of some is (Heb. 10:25). We must mark it well that low churchmanship is low Christianity, and low Christianity is a mark of low fidelity. When the church has to beg, entice, and compete on a popularity scale with the multitude of recreational or leisure options for the attention and faithful attendance of her constituency, then we are in a heap of trouble. And the church is currently in that battle, even though church attendance is said to be at one of its highest levels in history.

The reason for this anomaly is to be found in the third command, "serve the Lord." The problem with much of our contemporary churchgoing is that most prefer a larger church where they can get lost in the once-a-week crowd. It also has the advantage that our chances of being asked to take on a regular assignment are minimal. Most would not like to be tied down. But true service to God must replace the empty lip service of heartless worship offered only occasionally or even once a week. When other loyalties and interests usurp the place owed solely to God, then Baal worship exists just as surely as it did in Hezekiah's day. Some people's gods are their bellies; others, their jobs, families, books, friends, leisure time, vacation homes, television programs, sport teams, or ambitions (cf. Phil. 3:19).

If we persist in refusing to submit to the Lord, in taking lightly our need to come to the sanctuary or on insisting on serving our own self-interests ahead of serving God, then His fierce anger will break out against us corporately. It is a fearful thing to fall into the hands of the living God. We can ill afford to have God angry at us.

### Turn to Him with Unceasing Prayer or He Will Withdraw His Presence and Favor from Us (30:9)

In a clear echo of Solomon's dedicatory prayer in 1 Kings 8:50 (a verse that had been omitted in the parallel account of this same incident in 2 Chron. 6:39), Hezekiah urges all of Judah to pray for the forgiveness of God. Once again, now for the fourth and fifth times in this short passage of four verses, he uses the verb "to turn" as the burden of his message.

This role of an intercessor who acts as the mediator between God and one's community, church, family, institution, or nation is amply illustrated in such passages as Exodus 32-34, where Moses intercedes on behalf of his people, or even more dramatically, in Daniel 9:14-19. In the latter instance, Daniel used the first person plural, "us, we, our," at least thirty-nine times in his short prayer, signifying that he identified with his people as he confessed the sin of the whole group. Too frequently we have learned to pray only for ourselves, our families, and those closest to us—much on the order of the individualistic American who believes in looking out for number one. But who will pray for the larger groups if we do not? And how can we disassociate ourselves from the sin of the group? Is it not, as Daniel prayed, *our* sin and *our* confusion that has grieved God? We should learn to pray more in a corporate mode, as well as a personal mode, of confession of our own sin.

One important aspect of turning, then, is the return to prayer, not only for ourselves but also for the forgiveness of others, in an ever widening circle. And the promise of God can be found in His very name, as He announced to Moses in Exodus 34:6-7: He will be gracious and compassionate. We ought, therefore, to plead for His mercy.

Not only should our corporate praying be aimed at God's forgiveness, but we must also pray for restoration as well. Habakkuk prayed, "In wrath, remember mercy" (Hab. 3:2). So in addition to our returning to God, we must ask that He would return His favor to us. Only as God returns to His people, His church and His ministers, evangelists, and missionaries will we see the true dynamic for which we were created. But this will not come unless we make a complete reversal of directions and pledge ourselves, our hearts, minds, emotions, wills and energies totally to His service. We must "repent . . . and bring forth fruit worthy of repentance" (Matt. 3:2, 8). It must involve letting "everyone who names the name of Christ depart from iniquity" (1 Tim. 2:19).

Even those Ephesian believers who were seated with Christ in the heavenlies needed to hear the shout "Awake you sleeper and arise from the dead, and Christ shall give you light" (Eph. 5:14). What an astonishing evaluation of the spiritual condition of that church. But can any more be said about the condition of the contemporary evangelical church in the West?

If repentance is the condition of all of God's blessing, then we must do as Jeremiah urged, "Return, you backslid[er], only acknowledge your iniquity that you have transgressed against the Lord" (Jer. 3:12-13); and Joel, "Turn to me with all your heart . . . rip open your hearts and not your garments" (Joel 2:12-13); indeed, the Lord Himself through the prophet Malachi, "Return to me and [then] I will return unto you" (Mal. 3:7).

History will not be kind to those who demonstrate that they learn nothing from the past. The 1960s can and will be repeated if we do not return to God. I believe God has mercifully given us the years of tranquillity and peace in the 1970s and the first half of the 1980s because of the obedience of a few in the Body of Christ. Para-church groups and some God-given evangelists were responsible for picking up where the local church had all too frequently defaulted. There was a mighty sweeping of literally thousands into the family of God because the witness was faithfully and prayerfully given in the power of the Holy Spirit. But that avenue of ministry on campuses and in major crusades does not appear, for the moment, to be as fruitful as it once was in the United States and in Canada. The ball, as it were, is being bounced back again into the court of the local church. True, it was the local church, or at least its members, who cheerfully and extravagantly gave funds for the success of these para-church and evangelistic ministries. But it would appear that the next decade will belong to the gathered church in accordance with God's original design.

It is high time that we turn from our sin. It is time that we turn towards the Lord and espouse His service, His sanctuary, and submit to His name as the highest cause we could own.

Do you not long for authenticity and for the full power of the Lord Himself in your life and in the ministry of the church throughout the world? We have thrilled to every glimmer of success that the gospel has had so far. And yet, is it not time the hidden peoples of the world (including those in the United States) were found and exposed to the full light of the gospel? Is it not time that the truth-claims of the world's major world religions were exposed for what they are? Where is the God of Elijah? Is He not our God as well? And will not every religious leader need to appear before the tribunal of the living God in that final day? Where is the fear of God? Where is that boldness that comes from knowing the living God?

May a whole new wave of repentance and turning to God lead to a veritable downpour of His Spirit. And may this revived vitality lead to such widespread obedience that many will be swept into the kingdom of God in unprecedented numbers.

# 8

## It Is Time
## to Humble Ourselves Before the Lord:

### REVIVAL UNDER JOSIAH
### 2 Chronicles 34:1-33

**I**f the Spirit of God did not periodically send revival, this world would be in extremely sad shape. It is alarming to see how frequently the lessons learned by one generation are totally forgotten in another. But thanks be to God, He will not let His fallen children roam about in spiritual fatigue forever. Based on this marvelous record of intervention, there is always the hope and expectation that God will step into the present order of things, no matter how bleak and adverse the circumstances seem to be. Thus, all believers should have a deep expectation and a firm belief in the possibility of revival for their day.

It is true, of course, that some of the Old Testament revivals stressed the means that God was pleased to use to hasten revival. Care must be taken not to place too much emphasis on that word *means,* however, for it signifies little more than that God holds humanity responsible for such things as prayer and repentance. Means are not meritorious in and of themselves; revival is the work of God from beginning to end. Moreover, His Word also functions as one of the divinely designated means that God uses to drive individuals back to Himself. But it is not fair to pit that Word against Him in the heavy debates that tend to rage over the real source of revivals.

It is to be regretted that this debate has consumed so much of the energy of the believing community, energy that could have been invested in the work of revival as called for by Scripture. This is said neither to condone anti-intellectualism nor to imply that theology is unimportant or that there is not an important theological question involved in the debate. There is indeed a theology of revivals that has yet to be tackled, it is to be hoped by our generation. But there is no place for the kind of armchair theology of revivalism that refuses to put the discussion in the context of a working ecclesiology.

Theology was meant to be the servant of the church, not her uninvolved lord and dictator. Therefore, a theology of revivals will not only tackle questions about theology proper (doctrine of God) and soteriology (doctrine of salvation), but it will also root itself in an exegesis of the major teaching passages on the great revivals of the Bible. It will thereby help to bridge the gap of aiding practical theology, missions, and evangelism in working out strategies for putting that theology of revivals into practice.

It is time that our academies (seminaries and Bible schools) and churches said a firm no to the kind of abstract theologizing that refuses to dirty its hands with either the hard issue of interpreting the "chair passages" (*sedes doctrinae*) on revival throughout the Bible or the practical concerns of the ministry of Christ's church around the world. It is this hiatus more than any other factor that has made so many in the church suspicious of the abiding contributions and worthwhileness of the research of the academy. As one who has spent most of his life in the academy and who loves it, I call on my colleagues to move immediately in true biblical humility to rectify this suspicion by involving ourselves beyond the comfortable boundaries of the traditional range of our disciplines.

Now among the revivals that seem to lack secondary causes or human means that stress the individual's reception of the sovereign ministry of the Spirit of God, there is the revival under King Josiah. Prior to this revival there were no services at the sanctuary. Furthermore, the Bible had been lost, and hence little instruction could have been expected from that source. Was someone praying somewhere? Had someone memorized the Word of God, and was he teaching it to children, among whom was to be found the young prince Josiah? It is impossible to decide for certain among these alternatives.

But is it not possible then to make the point that there is only one ultimate source for all true revivals, and that is God Himself? Yes, it is, for just as we should not be frightened by the preparatory means that God has ordained to achieve revival, including His Word, prayer, repentance, seeking His face, turning from our wicked ways, and humbling ourselves, so we should not be shy in affirming the sovereignty of God in this whole work either. Without that doctrine, we cannot even get started in our discussion of revival.

But Josiah's revival has another noteworthy feature. It seems that this revival was especially recorded by the inspiration of God to highlight the requirement of *humbling ourselves* as one of the conditions of revival. The Hebrew verb translated "to humble ourselves" occurs in the Old Testament some thirty-six times, with half of the instances being secular and the other half being sacred. The secular use spoke of subduing or being subdued by an enemy, whereas the sacred use referred to bringing oneself low before God. It is interesting that the books of Samuel and Kings, which often contain material parallel to that in Chronicles, have only three examples of this verb. Two are connected with the external act alone, such as ripping one's clothes in grief, wearing sackcloth, or weeping and fasting. The only one of the three that overlaps material from Chronicles, however, is 2 Kings 22:19 (cf. 2 Chron. 34:11). Chronicles, on the other hand, accounts for fourteen of the total eighteen occurrences of this word used in a religious or sacred sense.[1] Furthermore, as pointed out earlier, it is this expression that figures prominently in the paradigm verse of 2 Chronicles 7:14. Clearly, then, it represents a distinctive concept in the theological formulation of the chronicler.

This is not the first time the concept of humbling oneself has been featured with the turnabout of a king, however. It would appear that the sequence of revivals we have been looking at in 2 Chronicles was bracketed by the chronicler by means of an *inclusio* that featured this term in the early days of the history he reports, just after the division of the kingdom from King Solomon. Thus, Rehoboam, the first Judean king after Solomon, was warned by the prophet Shemaiah that God had abandoned him to Pharaoh Shishak because he had seen fit to abandon God (2 Chron. 12:5). And instead of steeling themselves against the truthfulness of this warning, "the leaders of Judah and their king *humbled themselves* and said, 'The Lord is just'" (12:6). Accordingly, "when the Lord saw that they *humbled themselves*, this word came to Shemaiah: 'Because they have *humbled themselves*, I

1. These fourteen references are 2 Chron. 7:14; 12:6, 7 (twice), 12; 30:11; 32:26; 33:12, 19, 23 (twice); 34:27 (twice); 36:12. The root of this word is sometimes associated with "to bend the knee."

will not destroy them but will give them some deliverance'" (12:7). That is to say, even at this late date, when the invasion was already on, it still was not too late to turn in deep humility before the Lord God, who, in response, granted them a measure of relief. The Hebrew term above translated "some" means "for a little," or the like, and the rendering seems preferable to NIV's "soon give them deliverance." This view is sustained by the statement in 2 Chronicles 12:12, which repeats our key theological expression, that "because Rehoboam humbled himself, the Lord's anger turned from him, and he was not totally destroyed," adding, most significantly, "Indeed, there was some good in Judah."

The concept of humbling oneself is very close to the idea of turning to the Lord. Remember how the leaders and king confessed, "The Lord is just/righteous," when they humbled themselves? Not only did they make themselves low in the presence of God, but also they agreed that what He had done was "in the right" and richly deserved by them.

Again, biblical humility is a modesty that replaces vanity, pride, and arrogance. The person who has humbled himself or herself before God is one who is not wise in his or her own eyes, for so the wise writer of Proverbs counseled: "Do not be wise in your own eyes; fear the Lord and shun evil" (Prov. 3:7). The New Testament concurs: "Do not think more highly of yourself than you ought" (Rom. 12:3).

Third, the humble person recognizes that everything she or he may possess has been given by God. The question that Paul puts to us is, "What do we have that we have not received?" (1 Cor. 4:7). That in itself ought to be enough to keep us from boasting and flaunting whatever few skills may be ours.

But, finally, something more is required in this area of revival than a mere attitudinal reorientation: we need to turn to God with a contrite heart if we are to understand the biblical injunction to humble ourselves before God. David learned this truth when he cried out, "A broken and a contrite heart, O God, thou wilt not despise" (Ps. 51:17, KJV). Only by means of such a brokenness can God begin to remake us into that new person in Himself that we can and should be.

Examples of such humility are available in the biblical text. Moses is cited for his humility in Numbers 12:3, but this was no natural gift or lifetime experience. Nor was Moses what moderns often refer to as a wimp; he had naturally strong passions that needed to be conquered. In fact, his hatred of injustice and maltreatment of the oppressed was so strong that it led to several major sins early in his career, costing him an extension to his stay in God's school of hard knocks. But finally he surrendered his hot temper to God while retaining his God-given sense of fairness and justice for all.

A better example of biblical humility is Jesus. As the servant of the Lord described in Isaiah 53:4-10, He willingly submitted Himself to the plan and will of God. Philippians 2:6-8 explains the glory the preincarnate Son shared with the Father, yet He willingly gave it all up in order to do the Father's will. In imitation of the incarnate Son of God, Philippians 2:5 urges us to "let this mind-set be in you which was also in Christ Jesus." This is the same mind-set and frame of reference we must have in ourselves if we wish to see revival.

The apocryphal work Ben Sirach makes this astute observation: "The greater you are, the more you have to humble yourself in order to find favor with the Lord" (Sir. 3:18). This is not an inspired source, of course, but the observation is filled with truth. When we depend on our own wits or skills rather than on God's power, we become little gods to ourselves and to those around us. This is the opposite of the demand laid on us in Christ. It makes us resistant to the work of grace in our hearts, and there is no fertile field for the implantation of God's refreshing winds of revival.

"The fruit of humility," says the writer of Proverbs, "is the fear of the Lord, riches, honor, and life" (Prov. 22:4). Why then do we go about seeking on our own what we cannot and will not obtain apart from humbling ourselves under the mighty hand of God?

What then does it mean to humble ourselves? Franz Delitzsch summarized the matter succinctly when he concluded, "To subordinate oneself to God, and to give honour to Him alone, one must have broken his self-will, and come to the knowledge of himself in his dependence, nothingness, and sin."[2]

The theology of humbling oneself before God had been set in Leviticus 26:40-41. There Moses said: "But if they confess their sins and the sins of their fathers . . . then when their uncircumcised hearts are *humbled* and they pay for their sin, I will remember my covenant with Jacob." This passage provided the informing theology that lay behind 2 Chronicles 7:14. It must be carefully noted how significant a role both personal and collective, or corporate, confession has as a preparation to humbling ourselves under God. It is not enough for each of us to

---

2. Cf. Franz Delitzsch, *Biblical Commentary on the Proverbs of Solomon* (Grand Rapids: Eerdmans, 1950), 2:85.

confess his own personal sin; each of us must also confess the sin of the groups to which he belongs. This kind of confession is most scarce today, but it is most vital. Daniel prays this way in his famous prayer in Daniel 9, and so should we, because of our corporate identities and because of the command of the Lord that this must take place.

In accordance with the chronicler's teaching, it is high time that we humbled ourselves before the Lord. And if 2 Chronicles 12:6, 7, and 12 showed how this first took place in the life of Rehoboam at the beginning of the new kingdom of Judah, then 2 Chronicles 32:26; 33:12, 19, 23; 34:27; and 36:12 show the results of such humbling or of its delay or outright omission as the kingdom of Judah drew to a close. As noted above, the references form a type of *inclusio*, or bracketing, of the revivals of this book.

From among the final kings of Judah, God raised up young King Josiah to demonstrate the effectiveness of humbling ourselves under God. Accordingly, 2 Chronicles 34 calls on us to make three *abasements*, which may be stated as follows:

1. We must humble ourselves before our God (vv. 1-13).
2. We must humble ourselves before God's Word (vv. 14-28).
3. We must humble ourselves before God's people (vv. 29-33).

May the Lord grant to each of His own the ability to act with all speed and deliberateness in this important preparatory work of humility. And may the example of this young king's heart so stir us that we, too, would long for the same work of God in our lives.

### We Must Humble Ourselves Before God (34:1-13)

Josiah's reign over Judah began in 648 B.C. He was a mere eight years of age. At sixteen, "he began to seek after the God of David his father" (2 Chron. 34:3). As far as the record goes, Josiah had no examples or guides to follow. A very early influence, prior to his coming to the throne, may have been the prophetess Huldah (34:26-28). But he surely did not have any help from his grandfather Manasseh, who reigned for fifty-five years and led a most disgusting life of wickedness and evil. Not only did that king set up pagan high places for the worship of strange gods, he also copied "the abominations of the heathen" (2 Chron. 33:2). Following this weakening of the people, the kingdom of Judah was overrun by the Assyrians, who carried Manasseh off into captivity. Only then did he finally humble himself under God's mighty hand. But God heard his confession and brought him back to Jerusalem after he "knew that the Lord, He is God" (33:13). A weak reformation followed, but not enough to overthrow and unravel more than fifty years of wickedness. Josiah was approximately six years old at the time.

Next Manasseh's son, Amon, came to the throne, but he followed the wicked example of his father. After two years of ruling, his palace servants assassinated him. The people in turn ordered that those involved in this plot be put to death, for they were weary of all of the political corruption and intrigue. But no one seemed yet able to realize that their problems were moral and spiritual and had to do with their backslid condition.

Then the eight-year-old Josiah inherited the throne. He took as his model King David: "he walked in the ways of his father David" (34:2). The expression "to walk in the ways" signifies a life-style, in this case a path of practical holiness and righteousness. Solomon had urged, "Do not swerve to the right or to the left; keep your feet from evil" (Prov. 4:27). And Josiah took such a straight path, turning neither to the left or the right. Further, his thoughts, actions, and inclinations did not verge into left-wing or right-wing alliances.

It was early in his life that he sought the favor of God; he began in his sixteenth year (34:3). It must be observed that a tender heart is the only kind that can seek God and find Him, for hearts filled with sinfulness and indifference will remain impervious to any and all the works of God. The way of the transgressor is hard. But if revival is to come, God looks first of all for the tender, humble heart. This is the condition we must seek above all else if our hearts are to be as tender and open to the Lord as was Josiah's.

Josiah had many obstacles to overcome: his grandfather's long reign of wickedness, the sin and brutal murder of his father, the disrepair and disgrace of a dilapidated house of worship, the total loss of any awareness of the book of the law of God, and much else. But he found the Lord in spite of all of them.

We need a revival just as desperately as he did. For though it had been almost ninety years since God had last poured out His Spirit on that people, it has been eighty years (1905) since God has poured out His Spirit on us. What obstacle do we have that Josiah did not? That is answered for us by Ernest Baker. He noted:

> But though Josiah had [these obstacles] as a hindrance, there was one

great obstacle which he did not have to overcome. He was not confirmed to sin. There is nothing so hardening to the heart, and so blind-
ing to the eyes, and so searing to the conscience as sin. "Those who seek
me early shall find Me." Men who seek late in life, if they truly seek, will
find, but it will not be such easy work for them as it is for the young.[3]

Herein lies the greatest difficulty to seeking God: our sin. No wonder we are urged to seek His face early. This provides no excuse for
failing to take up the search in later years when youth has passed us
by. The time for that is always appropriate. But it will be more difficult
then, for we must humble ourselves and become as open and transparent as children if we wish to enter into the joys of the outpouring of
the Holy Spirit.

When Josiah turned twenty, he began a reform that purged the land
(34:3*b*). Every competitor of the real God was liquidated, including
altars, groves, images, and molten idols. In like manner we are warned
in the New Testament, "My little children, keep yourselves from idols"
(1 John 5:21), and, "Flee from idolatry my dearly beloved" (1 Cor.
10:14), and finally, "Mortify covetousness, which is idolatry" (Col. 3:5).

Not only did Josiah destroy these pagan installations, he scattered
the dust of the smashed idols over the graves of the idolaters. This is
significant, for even in death the guilt and horror of their religious
desecrations did not leave them. Their works, evil as they were, followed them beyond the grave.

Josiah also burned the dead bones of the false priests on their altars
(v. 5). By means of this action Josiah apparently unwittingly fulfilled
the prophecy of the man of God from Judah who had pronounced
judgment against wicked Jeroboam for his idolatrous altar: "O altar,
altar! This is what the Lord says: 'A son named Josiah will be born to
the house of David. On you he will sacrifice the priests of the high
places who now make offerings here, and human bones will be burned
on you'" (1 Kings 13:2). That was shortly after 931 B.C. Its fulfillment
occurred some three hundred years later in 628 B.C. Yet in this magnificent prophecy are included the name of the king, his act of dese-
crating the bones of these desecrators, and the rebuke for this golden
calf installation in the northern kingdom by a Davidic king.

In addition to seeking the Lord's favor in his youth, Josiah also did
His will in his youth (vv. 8-13). When Josiah was twenty-six, he began

---

3. Ernest Baker, *The Revivals of the Bible* (Capetown, South Africa: Miller, 1906), p. 83.

to repair the Temple. (The last comprehensive repair of God's house had been carried out by King Joash some 250 years before.) But even more significant, he moved to cleanse and to purify the land. This need for moral and spiritual cleanness was integral for the work of revival that was to come. The Old Testament doctrine of cleanness must not be confused with general cleanliness or with personal hygiene or the like. It signified the state of being ready or fit for the worship of or meeting with God. Haughty, proud, and arrogant men cannot worship, be blessed, or grow spiritually. They must humble themselves. The worship of God is one of the best contexts in which humbling of ourselves can take place.

We must ask ourselves, do we have tender hearts? Are we deeply moved by the moral and religious indifference of the populace about us? "Those who seek me early shall find me" (Prov. 8:17), says the Lord. That is, our quest for God and for doing His will must become an all consuming passion.

## We Must Humble Ourselves Before God's Word (34:14-28)

It was during the repair of the Temple that a most unusual discovery was reported: the book of the law. Can you imagine? The very people to whom God had graciously given His Word were the ones who had so neglected it that it was completely forgotten, lost from sight and memory. This has to be one of the crowning insults ever done by any people to the Lord. But we, too, "do err in not knowing the Scriptures" (Matt. 22:29). Before we begin throwing stones, we ought to remember: we evangelicals argue long and loud for the doctrine of the inerrancy of the Bible, but in our practice we shout something else.

"I have found the book of the law in the Temple of the Lord," exclaimed Hilkiah (34:15). And when it was brought to the king and read in his presence, he ripped open his robes in grief (vv. 18-19). More than anything else, this gesture substantiates the self-authenticating power of the Word of God. (Verse 27 tells us that the king also wept at its reading.)

If this book of the law was the book of Deuteronomy, as some contend, it could have been read in two or three hours. But if it contained the first five books of Moses, as is more likely, it probably consumed more like ten to twelve hours of the king's time. Imagine a modern audience, even an evangelical one, standing (or even sitting) and listening for twelve hours of Bible reading. But so great was the king's hunger for the Word of God and so frightening were the implications of the wrath of God, which almost certainly was impending on the nation, that every matter of state was put off in deference to this most pressing situation.

There is more here. There is the matter of the indestructibility of the Word of God. Autrey remarked,

> Despite the fact that God's people were fickle, that the priests and rulers were often godless, and that many of the perils threatened the destruction of the written word of God, it did not perish. It survived the indifference of its friends, the ravages of time, and the wilful plans of Satan. . . . One would almost be afraid for the Book if he should forget the perils through which the Word has come through the centuries. The Bible will survive; of this we have no doubt. But will the generation that loses knowledge of it? This is our concern.[4]

There is also the power of the Word of God, for the entrance of God's Word gives light. Thus, in spite of the previous reforms that Josiah had already introduced, when the entrance of God's Word came, he gained a greater understanding of what God had already begun to do. The proclamation, reading, and study of God's Word and meditation on it are absolutely essential in the lives of believers.

The basis of all true preaching and teaching of the Word of God is the fact that it has its source in the living Lord. Accordingly, the word of the prophets was "This is what the Lord, the God of Israel, says" (vv. 23, 24, 26). Too many in our day pronounce lying words in the name of the Lord that He has not spoken (cf. Jer. 29:23; Ezek. 13:7). There can be nothing more demoralizing than to speak or hear a message that is uncertain or whose authority is doubted. That is the number one plague of much liberal preaching today. But are evangelicals any better off? If we teach with the idea that this message has come from God but carelessly or openly refuse to obey it, are we any better off?

What Josiah focused on were the judgments of God. Indeed, the curses of God are just as true as are His blessings. We are taught to say "amen" to both. And if we know by experience that one is true, then we must also believe that the other is true as well.

When the king ordered, "Go and inquire of the Lord for me . . . what is written in this book" (v. 21), Hilkiah brought Huldah the pro-

---

4. C. E. Autry, *Revivals of the Old Testament* (Grand Rapids: Zondervan, 1960), p. 34.

phetess to him. Jeremiah had been ministering in Judah for five years, but God used a woman at this time. Thrice she assured the king that her authority was to be found only in the Lord Himself. The content of her message can be found in six expressions that parallel the contents of Deuteronomy 29. The phrases, which spoke of an impending disaster if the people did not confess their sin and humble themselves, are:

| | |
|---|---|
| v. 24 "all the curses written" | Deut. 29:20, 21, 27 |
| v. 25 "because they have forsaken me" | Deut. 29:25 |
| v. 25 "burned incense to other gods" | Deut. 29:26 |
| v. 25 "provoked me to anger" | Deut. 29:20, 23, 28 |
| v. 25 "[wrath] will be poured out" | Deut. 29:23, 28 |
| v. 25 "and will not be quenched" | Deut. 29:20 |

How massive is the heavy cloud of judgment that hangs over our heads if we do not humble ourselves and repent. But for the person whose heart is responsive to this word of judgment, there is great hope.

How important it is to respond to God's Word and to offer to Him a tender heart and receptive spirit. It is not sufficient to know that the Bible is God's Word or to argue for its inerrancy; we must, with a spirit of contriteness and humility, act on the basis of what it says. When we hear the Word proclaimed and applied to our times and people, surely we can sense that something is drastically wrong. Indeed, rather than leave him filled with indifference or unconcern, the Word of God will always overtake and arrest the humble and tenderhearted person, leading him or her on to obedience. O for more willing, responsive, and grateful hearts, minds, and feet.

God gives grace to the humble, and in due time He will once again exalt them (1 Pet. 5:5-6). Therefore, "Blessed are all those who weep, for they will laugh" (Luke 6:21). May we hear and respond to God's Word as never before, for it is time to humble ourselves under the Word of God.

## WE MUST HUMBLE OURSELVES BEFORE GOD'S PEOPLE (34:29-33)

Having abased ourselves before God and His Word, we must ask with our text, what about our abasement of ourselves before God's people? It is interesting that in this section the word "all" appears no less than eleven times in the original text. Every class of people whether "great or small" had to hear the words of the promise of God, for the Word was read in the hearing of all the people.

The king reconsecrated himself in his sacrifice to follow and to do with all his heart and soul all that God had spoken (v. 31). Leadership was given, therefore, to the people, who now joyously shared the Word as well.

The preaching of the Word produced three different results in the people. Some, like the king (v. 31), responded positively and decided to do all that was written in the law of God. Others took the pledge to act in accordance with that Word (v. 32) but without wholeheartedness, enthusiasm, or even any repentant remorse. What had been said of the king was not said of this group, for they did not agree to follow the Lord with all their heart and soul. They merely pledged, or literally, were "caused to stand" (i.e., as an act of pledging).

The third group also responded positively, and they joined in removing the detestable idols from all their territories. However, they served God only for the length of time that strong leaders were present (v. 33). It is noted that "they did not fail to follow the Lord, the God of their fathers, as long as Josiah lived." How odd that they should so quickly abandon the God of their fathers and for these Josiah years, at least, their God as well.

But for the moment we may rejoice that the revival had touched all. Standing beside "his pillar," the king had promised in the presence of God to renew His covenant and to follow God whether anyone else did or not (v. 31). In that sense he humbled himself not only in the presence of the Word of God and the God of the Word, but also before a watching nation. He did everything in his power to lead them back to the full experience of the blessing and joy of the Lord.

The brilliant career of this godly monarch was suddenly halted in one of the strangest episodes in the history of revelation. When he was thirty-nine, he went out to prevent Pharaoh Necho from going up to Carchemish on the Euphrates. Necho warned him that he should stay out of this matter, for he had no military intentions towards Judah or Israel. Furthermore, God had commanded him, Necho assured Josiah, to go up to this battle. But Josiah refused to listen, commented the writer of Chronicles under the inspiration of the Holy Spirit, "to what Necho had said at God's command" (2 Chron. 35:22). Thus, when Josiah, appearing in a disguise, interfered at the Megiddo pass, he was mortally wounded by the archers, and a brilliant, godly career came to an end just prior to the awful days of the end of the empire.

Josiah died in 609 B.C. Daniel and his friends were taken into Babylonian captivity in 606, followed by Ezekiel in 598 B.C. The end came when the Babylonians returned for a third time in 586 B.C. and destroyed everything, including Jerusalem and the Temple. Not more than a dozen years earlier (621 B.C.), however, God had promised during the repair of the Temple and the finding of the book of the law that because Josiah had humbled himself before Him and because he had humbled himself before His Word (v. 27), "I will gather you to your fathers and you will be buried in peace. Your eyes will not see all the disaster I am going to bring on this place and on those who live here" (v. 28). And so it happened just as God promised, for Josiah died prior to those dreadful days, even though the circumstances under which he died were unusual.

If we search for a reason for Israel's final disaster, we may turn to 2 Kings 23:26. The writer, after detailing the marvelous finding of the book of the law and the revival under Josiah, remarks that "still the Lord did not turn from the fierceness of His great wrath, by which His anger was kindled against Judah, because of all that Manasseh had done to provoke Him to anger." The destiny of Jerusalem and Judah was fixed, for the cup of their iniquity had filled so full that not even Josiah's reform could ultimately stay the ominous judgment that was sure to come. The most that he could have done was to offer a brief respite from it.

What then is our response? Are we moved at all when we view our sins against the crystal clear character of God? If so, then why will we not abase ourselves in the presence of this wonderful Lord? Again, are we still able to be taught by God's Word, and do we find it to be the source of our every authoritative word from heaven? If so, then why do we not obey its marvelous commands? It is time to humble ourselves in the presence of God, God's Word, and God's people, whom we wish to serve and to stimulate to righteousness, and before whom we live. We have too much pride, arrogance, and haughtiness; we mostly have reason for anything but these responses.

God searches for those who are "poor in the realm of the spirit," for those who have gone into spiritual bankruptcy in order that they might be revived from above and experience times of refreshing from the Lord.

May He grant us the strength of our convictions and mourning for our sin and the sin of our nation. May we learn at the end of such humility of soul and body that "the Lord [indeed] is righteous."

# 9

# It Is Time to Renew the Work of God:

## REVIVAL UNDER ZERUBBABEL
## Haggai 1; Zechariah 1:1-6

**F**ollowing the revival under Josiah, God's people had drifted back into degradation and sin, developing the seeds of wickedness planted during the administration of Manasseh. Thus it became necessary for them to learn through adversity what they had refused to learn by responding to the Word of God. Accordingly, Judah spent seventy years in captivity in Babylon, stripped of the comforts of Jerusalem. Mercifully God had once more intervened by putting it into the heart of the pagan king Cyrus to release the people if they so wished and to aid them in reestablishing their place of worship. This had been foretold by Isaiah (Isa. 44:28), who predicted not only Cyrus's two great merciful acts but the name of this Medo-Persian monarch as well.

And so it was that in 538 B.C. the decree was signed and a small band of less than fifty thousand persons returned to Jerusalem after seventy years of captivity. Some estimate that this represented less than one out of every six Jews in Babylon. Even more discouraging, this tiny group returned with very little evidence of a genuine spiritual work in their hearts. Ernest Baker places the first of four postexilic revivals at this point of the return. But frankly, the opening three chapters of Ezra do not indicate any great stirring, either of confession or of the Spirit of God. It is true that they immediately began construction on the Temple by laying its foundations in the second month after their arrival, but discouragement quickly set in, and the work ground to a halt. During the next sixteen years, not an ounce of energy was expended on this project, and the people were content to let the matter drop. That hardly seems like the result of a revival. Instead, it is an argument for one to come. Finally, 101 years after the last revival under Josiah (104 years had elapsed between Josiah's revival and Hezekiah's), Haggai and Zechariah both came preaching the word of the Lord in 520 B.C.

Ezra 5-6 describes the condition of things at that time. Zerubbabel, the grandson of the Judean king Jehoichin, who had been taken into captivity in 598 (2 Kings 24:15), became "governor" and led the first return in 537/6 B.C. His designation as governor was a reminder of the Babylonian appointment. Even his name was a loan word from Akkadian/Babylonian into Hebrew. That is, Zerubbabel was also known as Sheshbazzar (Ezra 1:8; 5:14), for the same work said to be done by Zerubbabel in Ezra 3:8 is said to have been done by Sheshbazzar in Ezra 5:16.

Zerubbabel belonged to the continuing line of David. The demonstration of this is somewhat involved and not crystal clear at all points, but the main facts are these. Jehoiachin had five sons, who are known to us mainly from the written tablets found in the famous Ishtar gate complex in Babylon. It would appear that they were made eunuchs, and thus the royal line of David was threatened (Isa. 39:7). Consequently, Jehoiachin adopted the seven sons of Neri, a descendant of David through Nathan, one of Solomon's brothers (1 Chron. 3:5). Thus Solomon's line ceased at this point, failing with Jehoiachin as Jeremiah had predicted: "Write this man off as childless, a man who shall not succeed in his days; none of his offspring shall . . . sit . . . on the throne of David" (Jer. 22:30). But Neri's oldest son, Shealtiel, died childless, and so his brother Pedaiah performed the rite of levirate marriage (Deut. 25:5-10); from his loins came the new Davidite, Zerubbabel. Hence Zerubbabel was the legal son of Shealtiel, and thus of David, but the actual son of Pedaiah and thus also of David.

Suddenly in the midst of his governorship (520 B.C.), God sent two prophets, Haggai and Zechariah, to rekindle the vision and hearts of the people. It was the sixth month. The season for summer fruits was now ended, and the time of harvest was over. We can almost hear the mournful sigh of Jeremiah, "The summer is over and we are not saved" (Jer. 8:20). Surely some must have remembered the famous pun on the Hebrew word for "summer," which also sounds like the

Hebrew word for "end," used by the prophet Amos (Amos 8:1-12). Would this truly be the end for the people? What did God have in mind by sending these prophets at this stage in the year and after sixteen years of no Temple, no worship, and no concern for spiritual things? There was enough solemn precedent from the past to alert any who had the least amount of spiritual sensitivity left in their bones.

The message of Haggai, which came first in this new stirring and is recorded in Haggai chapter 1, stressed four *ways* in which the work of God could be renewed in their day if the people would but respond. They are:

1. Refuse to blame the providence of God (vv. 1-2).
2. Set priorities for the work of God (vv. 3-6).
3. Get involved in the work of God (vv. 7-12).
4. Receive the enablement of God (vv. 13-15).

The prophet Habakkuk had once prayed, "In the midst of the years, renew your work, O Lord" (Hab. 3:2). The Lord was about to do just that by means of His two messengers. Therefore Haggai challenged God's people to face up to the weakness of their excuses.

### REFUSE TO BLAME THE PROVIDENCE OF GOD (1:1-2)

On August 29, 520 B.C., according to the nomenclature of our calendar, the Lord sent Haggai to challenge the people of God. This was the first time in this postexilic era that the voice of God was heard through a prophet. It is significant that his arrival is not dated in terms of either the Davidic succession or the promise that God had made to Israel. Rather it was reckoned as occurring "in the second year of King Darius," a ruler of the Gentiles. The times of the Gentiles had arrived.

The message itself was simple and direct. It was what the Lord of Hosts had observed: "This people say, 'The time has not yet come to build the Lord's house.'"

The distance that had come to exist between God and His people is suggested by one of the rare uses in the Old Testament of the expression "this people" to describe them. Surely it was a mark of the divine displeasure. Previously, even under the most difficult of circumstances, the Lord had referred to Judah and Israel as "my people." But they had definitely strained their relationship with Him, and the demonstrative pronoun indicated that there was a gap of major proportions existing as a result of their sin.

Telling was the lament that the time had not yet come to take up the work of rebuilding the Temple. Yet the people had found time and materials to effect the rebuilding of their own homes. Was not this only an excuse for delaying this job now for sixteen years? Think of it: one whole generation had been raised without any provision made for the corporate worship of the living God.

Furthermore, when the people used the word "time," they were saying in effect, "If God had wanted us to rebuild the Temple, He should have seen to it that we were better off than we are at the present." That is, the word "time" was only a stand-in word for God, and the people were hiding their own delinquencies behind it. But that was the problem. The reason they gave was a mere pretext for their own laziness and selfish reinvestment of time and interests. Yes, they were going to get around to rebuilding the Temple, but not now. There were other things that had to happen first. For example, relations with the Persians had not yet been normalized. Furthermore, they had not yet recovered sufficiently from the long years of the exile. They likewise probably reasoned that they were in a period of economic depression or inflation, and, finally, that these things just took time.

But to the one who wants to do what is right, the time is always present and available. It is we who are ingenious when it comes to inventing excuses or hiding behind our failures to respond to the Word of God. Therefore, we must recognize in the general national situation the rebuke of God. We must refuse to toy with the symptoms of the current distresses and go rather to their direct spiritual causes. As Matthew Henry advised, "It is bad enough to neglect our duty, but it is worse to vouch providence for the patronizing of our neglect."[1] No, the time was more than ripe for doing the work of God, even as it is now for us as well. We, too, must stop making excuses, for how will the reviving work of God ever begin when our hearts exhibit such desperate need of revitalizing?

But there is a second way in which we can renew the work of God in our times and prepare for revival.

1. Matthew Henry as cited by Richard Wolff, *The Book of Haggai* (Grand Rapids: Baker, 1967), p. 27.

## SET PRIORITIES FOR THE WORK OF GOD (1:3-6)

Again the word of the Lord came to this prophet, and he asked, "Is it time for you to live in your paneled homes?" The point was not that nice homes are a mark of wickedness or that believers would be better served by rejecting all material things. The Bible clearly teaches a full theology of culture and the proper use of things in all their beauty and mundaneness. But there is the issue of priorities. We must put God's work ahead of our work.

In this case the choice had to do with building the Temple. The religious condition of the people's hearts could be seen by their attitude towards this need. Actually, it could have come in the form of any task to do for the Savior; this was only the most pressing need of the moment. In fact, the flagrant and patent evidence that Yahweh was not their Lord was the dilapidated state of the Temple, which remained as it had for the past sixteen years and for the almost seventy years of their captivity. It was a disgrace and an object of scorn for all who passed by its burned-out ruins. The pagans mocked and hissed with glee over the remains of the place formerly inhabited by the so-called Lord of the universe.

To neglect God's house was tantamount to treason against Him, for no matter what the verbal level of affirmation of trust in Him, the plain fact was that no one cared in the least what He said. Ultimately this attitude was to invite God's rejection of all their labors.

If times were hard, and there was no denying that they were, why had Judah not cried out to God for help to do this work of building? And furthermore, if they were really so poor, how had they been able to spend so much on themselves? That was the real point in bringing up their paneled or wainscoted homes. (We are not entirely certain what the adjective means. The Septuagint rendered it "vault-roofed," the Vulgate "panel-ceiled," and the Chaldee "covered with cedar boards." Note Jeremiah 22:14, where paneled homes of cedar were painted with vermilion.)

Meanwhile the Temple of God remained "a ruin" (v. 4). The Hebrew word is similar to the one translated "Sinai," which we also know as Mt. Horeb. *Horeb* means a desert, dry place, or ruin. Therefore the prophet was making a pointed play on these words in verses 9 and 11 when he quoted God as saying, "Because my house is a 'ruin,' therefore I have called for a 'ruin,' or drought, on your crops." The subject deserved earnest reflection (v. 5) similar to that mentioned in Lamentations 3:40: "Let us search and try our ways and turn again to the Lord." In short, the people were called to assay whether anything was to be gained by trying to outreach God.

It was time for God's people to evaluate where this reversal of priorities had got them. Were they sowing more and harvesting less? Were they eating more and enjoying it less? Were they drinking more and enjoying it less? Were they earning more and accumulating less? The answer was yes to all four of these questions, but why? In the Hebrew text the string of verbs in verse 6 is in what is called the infinitive absolute construction. This construction adds force to the timeless aspect of the principle involved: it is universal for all times, seasons, and countries. Simply put, the principle is that no one cheats God without cheating himself at the same time. But the reverse truth is just as clear, "Seek first the kingdom of God and His righteousness and all these things will be added unto you" (Matt. 6:33).

There is a definite connection between the moral and spiritual condition of a people and their material and economic condition. This connection is not only found here in verses 3-6 but throughout the Old Testament. It is unfortunate that many moderns who are familiar with many of the secondary explanations for natural and economic events feel that these are sufficient. But there is also a moral cause for the conditions of drought and plenty. This connection goes all the way back to the Fall in Eden, where the ground was cursed for the sake of man. Likewise the world was flooded because of humanity's wickedness, and country after country has been expelled from its land for lack of righteousness and justice. Only when Christ returns will the created order be restored to that for which it groans and travails (Rom. 8:19-22).

It was time for them to renew God's work and for a whole new order of priorities to be established if revival was ever to come. The same is true of us today.

### GET INVOLVED IN THE WORK OF GOD (1:7-12)

Verse 7, which again stresses the importance of these matters, is reminiscent of verse 5. The title "Lord of Hosts" is never used of deity in the Pentateuch, Joshua, or Judges. Its first appearance is in 1 Samuel 1:3. But it is the favorite expression of the prophets from that time on. Of its 300 occurrences in the Old Testament, 247 of them are in the prophets, and when the size of the books is taken into account, the greater proportion of them appear in the postexilic period. Haggai's little book has 14 examples, Zechariah has 53, and Malachi has 24 for a total of 91 of the prophets' 247 examples. The meaning of "Lord of Hosts," that is, Master of the heavenly and earthly armies, is that He is the absolute sovereign with invincible might, holding both terrestrial armies (1 Sam. 17:45) and celestial armies of angels (Ps. 24:7-10) at His beck and call.

The purposes of obedience are set forth in verse 8: "so that I may take pleasure in [that work]." Thus it is not that God is pleased or impressed with buildings per se, but insofar as that building represents the attempt to express praise and worship to God, to that degree it brings Him pleasure and magnifies His name. Therein lies the true motivation for all acts of service to the living God.

It is a matter of interest that it was necessary for the people to go up to the mountains to cut timber and to bring it down to build the Temple. Sixteen years ago they had been given lumber for this purpose. What had happened to it in the meantime? Had it just rotted in the piles where it was placed when the original project had been abandoned after the foundations had been laid? Or had the people stolen the timber that should have been used for the house of God and used it instead to construct their own homes? Whatever the explanation, they must now replace it if the project was to go on.

In addition to the doxological purposes of our obedience, this section also deals with the costs of our disobedience. When God's work had to go begging for lack of interest, punishment fell, affecting the very ground itself. Once again, Scripture repeatedly underlines the intimate connection between man's performance and nature's productivity. The costs are dramatic. There were shortages in materials, shortages in goods, shortages in food, and shortages in wages. Furthermore, it was God who called for this drought on the land according to verse 11. If we mistake this connection in our current assessment of society and its problems, we will miss also in rectifying the situation to any significant degree.

Verse 12 is one of those rare verses in the Bible that indicates that the preaching of God's Word had an immediate and wonderful effect. It celebrates the beauty of obedience, because all the people along with the leadership obeyed the voice of the Lord. The "fear" of the Lord mentioned here is an attitude of wholehearted trust and glad submission to the living Lord. It meant a turning from evil ("The fear of the Lord is to depart from evil," Prov. 9:10; cf. Prov. 8:13) and a seizing hold of the Lord by faith (Ps. 2:11). Only by meeting these conditions can the work of God break out in our own hearts and in a needy world.

The people believed because God had sent His prophet. May we never forget that the Word of God, joined by the convincing and convicting power of the Holy Spirit, always will be the dynamite of God (1 Thess. 1:4).

### RECEIVE GOD'S ENABLEMENT TO DO THE WORK OF GOD (1:13-15)

Many will complain in exasperation, "But I am so weary and so unable to do anything more. How can I receive this challenge to renew the work of God? Already I believe much better than I practice. How will one more challenge help me? Is there no word of comfort in the gospel other than this repeated emphasis on the need to come clean in confession to God and to have His work renewed in my heart?"

The good news from this text, Old Testament text that it is, is that for those who responded to the call there was immediately available the enabling power of the Lord. The most comforting word for these hurting sinners was "I am with you, says the Lord" (v. 13). Nothing strikes more hope and encouragement into the hearts of God's people than this phrase. It is too bad that we have ruined the statement by our trite use of the preposition *with*. We say to others, "Yes, I am with you, and I am behind you," but we never say how *far* behind we will be, nor do we make it immediately clear that we are with them only in a *general* way. But when the Lord uses the word, He means that He is personally, dramatically, and powerfully standing alongside us, no matter what the assignment. There is the real difference. Thus we will never be left to do a solo performance, for there will be two who teach the class, not just one; there will be two who play the piano or organ, not just one; there will be two who witness, not just one. That is what the Lord means when He says, "I am with you." That is enough to revolutionize how most of us think of Christian service or the prospect of success in any Bible study, youth group, evangelistic mission, or overseas task that confronts the toughest opposition imaginable.

More than this, the Lord also promised to stir up the spirit of the leadership and the spirit of the people so that they together would have a mind to work. And so it was on September 21, 520 B.C.—the people came together to get on with a job that had been sinfully neglected since 536 B.C. How beautiful is the work of God on our hearts when it is received with the kind of joy manifested here.

As if to reinforce this message or to extend it deeper into the population of the community, God sent the prophet Zechariah in November of 520 B.C. He gave (Zech. 1:1-6) "one of the strongest and most intensely spiritual calls to repentance to be found in the OT."[2] The prophet pointed out that God was extremely angry with the wicked. Nothing can make this a pretty doctrine. Of course God is a God of love, but we must not conceal the fact that He is also the God of wrath. It is a sure sign of a sickly piety when men and women are willing to hear nothing but the love of God. Verse 2 is very emphatic on this point, for it has a triple emphasis on anger—and the people knew this was so, for after all, what was the Exile all about?

However, all was not lost. Repentance is the condition for all of God's blessings (v. 3), for when individuals and significant numbers of people in a nation turn to God, He in turn will turn to them. "Return to me, says the Lord of hosts, *so that* I may return to you" (v. 3).

Indeed, we are responsible for the lessons taught to us by history. Four times the text refers to the fathers (vv. 2, 4, 5, 6). But even they passed on, and where were they now? This question accented the brevity of such spiritual opportunities as Zechariah was offering, and the dangerous situation that they brought (v. 5). Both the ministry of the prophets, whom many thought they would never be rid of, and the fathers' longevity were all too short.

But, wonder of wonders, in spite of all this change and transience, there remains the permanence of the Word of God and the invincibility of God's purposes for the ages (v. 6). Thus, what the Lord had both threatened and promised, He has done.

The conclusion is before us once again. It is abundantly clear that we must stop giving to God the scraps of our time and energy. It will do no good to pretend that life has dealt us a blow and therefore we cannot do otherwise than what we are doing now. The truth is as T. V. Moore put it: "The events of life are hieroglyphics in which God records his feelings towards us, the key to which is found in the Bible."[3]

For those who long to fight inflation, blight, crop failure, shrinking monetary values, and spiritual depression around the world, this text urges us to repent and turn back to the Lord and set our priorities straight. We must stop pretending we are too poor or that the time is

2. G. L. Robinson, "Zechariah, Book of," *The International Standard Bible Encyclopedia*, ed. James Orr et al. (Grand Rapids: Eerdmans, 1952), 5:3137.
3. T. V. Moore, *Haggai, Zechariah, and Malachi* (New York: Carter, 1856), p. 66.

not quiet propitious, for in that day our possessions will become tongues that will wag and tell on us. Now is the time and now is the right moment to call out to God, regardless of how wretched our situation may be.

For those who will respond, the stirring that God will effect will lead to a whole new work of the grace of God in their lives. May that work of God come in our lives, and may the life of the nation be renewed once again.

# 10

## It Is Time to Rejoice in the Lord:

### REVIVAL UNDER EZRA AND NEHEMIAH
### Nehemiah 8

**"T**his is the longest of all the revival stories in the Bible," commented Ernest Baker.[1] And it belongs to the same general period as the one under Zerubbabel with Haggai and Zechariah.

There were three different groups that returned from Babylon under three different leaders. We have already discussed the first, which was led by Zerubbabel in 537/6 B.C. This was the group that returned to Palestine filled with fervor and a deep desire to blot out the blemish of the desecration of the Temple of God. The foundations were laid, but, alas, there was so much weeping about its puny size in comparison with the previous Temple and there was so much opposition that the work ground to a halt. And so it remained for sixteen long years, until God stirred the people with a revival under the preaching of Haggai and Zechariah in 520 B.C.

Eighty years after the first return, the scribe Ezra led another return of exiles in 457 B.C. This return is described in Ezra 7-10. There can be no doubt that Ezra was a godly man. Furthermore, God used him significantly to effect a great change in the lives of the returnees. But it is difficult to say whether this should be counted as one of the great revivals of the Old Testament or as more of a reformation. Ernest Bak-

---

1. Ernest Baker, *The Revivals of the Bible* (Capetown, South Africa: Miller, 1906), p. 117.

er argues that it was a genuine revival; in fact he finds four revivals in this postexilic period where we are only arguing for two.

The key to Ezra's life was that he "had set his heart to study the law of the Lord, and to do it, and to teach His statutes and ordinances to Israel" (Ezra 7:10). It is no wonder, then, that God used him, for he had made up his mind and prepared his heart not only to enter into a study of the Word of God but also to do what it commanded and to teach others to do the same. That is the mark of a real disciple. Moreover, "the hand of God was upon Ezra for good" (Ezra 7:6, 9, 28; 8:18, 22, 31).

When Artaxerxes granted him permission to return to Jerusalem with a group of Jews, he gave him wide-ranging authority to set up formal study of the Word of God with penalties for those who would not obey. But when they came to the most dangerous portion of their journey at the river Ahava, Ezra had the people pause for three days in prayer and fasting, for they would now be exposed to wild animals and bands of robbers (they were carrying the silver and golden vessels previously taken from the Temple by Nebuchadnezzar weighing about twenty-five metric tons). Because Ezra had testified to the Persian monarch that God was able to protect them, he felt embarrassed to ask for any protection from his army, even though Ezra had no trained soldiers or fighters in his group. But they "humbled themselves before the[ir] God" (Ezra 8:21), and God answered them by placing His hand on them for His good.

This characteristic phrase of Ezra and Nehemiah, "the hand of the Lord," meant five things for Ezra, and it has the same set of meanings for us: "It guides; and we are obedient to its leadings. It protects, and none shall pluck us out of His hand. It also provides. It brings help to us as required. And it strengthens us for work. It gives us confidence that when guided by Him we shall not fail."[2]

Ezra arrived safely without a military escort. But when he heard about the life-style of the Jews who had returned eighty years before and how they had amalgamated with the pagans in marriage and habits, Ezra was dumbfounded. He sat speechless for a whole day (Ezra 9:1-4). How could the blessing of God be expected on such backsliding?

All who trembled at the law of God joined with Ezra in mourning over the sin of the nation. At the time of the evening sacrifice, he arose

2. Ibid., p. 114.

and poured out his heart to God but asked for nothing. He could only confess the nation's sin, weep over it, and acknowledge that they were embarrassingly exposed to every sort of attack from almost everyone because of it. Then it was that a certain Shechaniah rose to suggest that although it was true that they had broken the covenant and married unbelievers, there still was hope in spite of this (Ezra 10:2).

Three days later the remnant gathered at Jerusalem in a heavy rainstorm, trembling because of their guilt and because of the rain (Ezra 10:9). When Ezra confronted them with their sin (Ezra 10:11), the people responded: "It is so; we have done as you have charged" (v. 12). Arrangements were made for the orderly disposition of these matters as quickly as possible.

Was this a revival? Possibly so, for it had the elements of humbling oneself, confession, turning from sin, and seeking God's face as revealed in His law. However, it was very limited in the scope of issues that it dealt with: intermarriage with unbelievers. Of course, it is true that generally it is a single issue on which the need for a revival is precipitated, but the factor that decides whether a reformation or a revival has occurred is the effect it has on the whole inner disposition and hearts of the people. It is this latter feature that is strangely missing from this revival. But the point is not worth fighting over, for it is purely a problem in categorization. The people's intermarriage with unbelievers was blocking God from fully opening His hand of blessing on the life of the community. God can be praised for such a uniform resolution of this key issue, which restored the blessing that had been so evidently on Ezra and on those who had trusted God in the matter of their return.

The third and final return took place under Nehemiah in 445 B.C. There is no question that a great revival took place in his days, some seventy-five years after the one led by Haggai and Zechariah.

Nehemiah was not looking for a task, for he was employed already in one of the highest positions in the land, especially for a captive. He was the king's "cupbearer" (Neh. 1:11). This did not mean he was a headwaiter or food-taster; his was a cabinet post in the upper echelons of government. But this all changed quite unexpectedly and suddenly when he received a visit from his brother, who brought a most discouraging report about the status of the city walls, gates, and returnees in Jerusalem. Trouble abounded on every hand, and in addition, the walls of the city and its gates had been (apparently) freshly burned once again. The city stood exposed to any and every attack (1:2-3).

This was distressing news to Nehemiah, for when he heard this awful report, he sat down and wept and mourned for days (1:4).

He began to fast and pray, beseeching God to remember His promises to the patriarchs (1:5) and to Moses (1:8; cf. Deut. 4:25-31 and Lev. 26:33). His prayer continued constantly from what would be around our Thanksgiving time in November until our Easter in March/April. During this time God prepared Nehemiah's heart to be part of the solution. Nehemiah was forming a plan to make his plea on behalf of this situation to King Artaxerxes. Even as he made his request to the Persian monarch, however, he offered a quick prayer to God (Neh. 2:4). To the delight of Nehemiah, Artaxerxes granted him his request, and thus the hard task commenced.

No doubt it took a lot of sacrifice to give up the influential position that he, an outsider, had achieved in the government. Nehemiah could easily have argued that it was important for him to stay where he was; look what this could possibly mean in his representing the interests of his fellow Jews. After all, the problem over in Jerusalem could be cared for by almost anyone. It affected such a small number of people at the time; surely there was another person just as qualified as he was. But we hear none of these arguments from Nehemiah. Instead, he was moved by the Spirit of God while he continued to call out to God for relief from this open shame of His city. God pointed to him, and he agreed to go and serve.

The story of how Nehemiah returned with a third group of exiles, how he conceived a plan to rebuild the walls, and the opposition he faced is all recorded in the book that bears his name (Neh. 2-7). After he had been in the razed city for only three days (2:11-12), he had formulated a plan by which the task could be carried out. The job was completed in a record fifty-two days (6:15), for nothing can stop God's servants or the work of God when it is done in God's way, using His methods.

Chapters 8-10 occupy a central position in the book of Nehemiah, taking up as they do the issue of the people's spiritual status before God now that they had been given the security of the walls and gates around them and there was no immediate fear of being exposed to the whims of every robber, marauder, or army. Indeed, all stood ready at last for dedication, but there was a prior matter to be cared for. More is needed for the sustenance of any nation, especially the weak, struggling country of refugees that Judah was at this time. They needed a deeper spiritual life. That life could only come from the Lord and could only be mediated through His Word, prayer, confession, humbling themselves before God, and deliberately turning from their wicked ways. Before the people could dedicate the walls and gates of the city, it was first necessary for them to reconsecrate themselves. Here, too, they needed leadership. This leadership also came from Nehemiah when he convened all the people, on the feast of trumpets (Num. 29:1-6), in a holy convocation.

Nehemiah and Ezra led the people in spiritual renewal just as effectively as they had led them in returning to the land or in giving them administrative guidance. And Nehemiah 8 records one of the most joyful and spectacular celebrations of the work of God known in the Old Testament. This chapter sets forth three *ways*, exemplified by the exiles who had returned and finished rebuilding the walls and gates, that God's people can begin to rejoice in the Lord, namely,

1. By satisfying our hunger for the Word of God (vv. 1-8)
2. By finding the joy of the Lord is our strength (vv. 9-12)
3. By uniting to proclaim God's faithfulness (vv. 13-18)

Consider them with me one by one.

## SATISFYING A HUNGER FOR THE WORD OF GOD (8:1-8)

More desperate than their need for protecting the walls around their cities was the people's need for a garrisoning of their hearts and minds in the living Lord. Finally an insatiable hunger, which apparently had been suppressed all these years, broke out with an abandon that seemed as if it would never be filled. As if drawn by a magnet, they came by the droves: men, women, and all who were old enough to understand (8:2). There at the Water Gate on the east side of town the people assembled. Their motive was to keep the new moon of the seventh month, the Feast of Trumpets, or Rosh Hashanah, as a feast of thanksgiving for God's gracious assistance and enablement in building the wall. This goodness of God instinctively led them to hunger to hear from God's Word.

A large wooden platform had been constructed (8:4) so all the people in the assembly could see and hear the reading of the Word. The scene was memorable: There was Ezra in the middle of the platform flanked by thirteen priests, six on his left hand and seven on his right. Acting on the request of the people, he brought the scroll of the law of

God (8:2) and opened it in front of all (8:5). Then a most amazing thing happened. When he opened the scroll of the Word of God, immediately all the people stood (v. 5). This was more than a token gesture, for they remained standing for the duration of the reading, which consumed most of the morning, except for those times when they broke into small groups for explanations and questions. The practice is a most God-honoring practice.

I have often pondered the significance of our present periods of standing during church services. They seem to be little more than routine signals, indicating that certain marks have been reached in the program, or opportunities to stretch our legs in order to keep us from falling asleep. How much more meaningful this simple gesture could be if it were connected with a desire to show thanksgiving, respect, and honor to the God of heaven. We need a holistic theology of worship that provides a new basis for all acts of standing in our services. And surely one of the reasons that should be placed high on the list is to show respect, alertness, joy at, and full attention to the hearing of the Word of God.

Also, too frequently we apologize for any reading from Scripture that requires .more than a few minutes of this traditionally hour-long service. But why should we be so miserly? Should we allow announcements, hymns written by uninspired human poets, or other trappings to successfully occupy more time than the Word of God? Is this not an additional indicator that we need to ask God for a new hunger for His Word, even as these people exhibited?

Six hours each day were consumed in Bible reading and explanation. Ezra read "from the light," that is, from early in the morning (around 6:00 A.M.; v. 3) until mid-day. In the midst of these long sessions of the reading of God's Word, they broke up into smaller groups so that thirteen Levites could explain to the people what they had just heard (vv. 7-8). Thus it was that the famine of the hearing of the Word of God finally ended (cf. Amos 8:11, "Behold the days are coming says the Lord God, when I will send a famine on the land, not a famine for bread, but [a famine] of hearing the words of the Lord"). This famine was not assuaged merely with the hearing of these words, as if they were somehow magical in their import or effect, for the hunger persisted until the people understood what was read. Thus the thirteen Levites followed Ezra's reading of the law with an exposition of that passage (v. 8).

Some modern interpreters say that the thirteen Levites translated the Hebrew text into the new lingua franca of the exiles: Aramaic. But this view does not make sense in light of the fact that at the same time other portions of the Old Testament were being received in Hebrew, such as Haggai, Zechariah, Malachi, 1 and 2 Chronicles, Ezra, Nehemiah, and Esther. It hardly seems possible that these books should have been written and preserved in the Hebrew script if this was no longer the language of the people. In fact, the Hebrew word around which this debate swirls does not mean "to translate" in Nehemiah 8:8, but "to explain," as it does in the Targums. Accordingly, The Levities "read from the books, from the law of God, *explaining the meaning*, giving the sense of what they read."

What a great formula for success. If only those who teach and preach God's Word today would stick to the text of Scripture with the same degree of intensity and proceed through the Scriptures in the same orderly manner, we too would have a great revival from God.

As they made their explanations, they pointed to the text of Scripture. For some time now I have been urging my students to "hold your finger on the text" as they preached, so that if they gestured with the right hand, then they should have the left hand on the text, and if they reversed hands for gesturing, so they should also reverse hands for holding the spot in the text they were commending to the whole group of believers to receive.

Too often the Bible is little more than a book of epigrammatic sayings or a springboard that gives us a rallying point around which to base our editorials. But where did we get the audacious idea that God would bless our opinions or judgments? Who wants to hear another point of view as an excuse for a Bible study or a message from the Word of God? Who said God would bless our stories, our programs for the church, or our ramblings on the general area announced by the text? Surely this is a major reason why the famine of the Word continues in massive proportions in most places in North America. Surely this is why the hunger for the teaching and proclamation of God's Word continues to grow year after year. Men and women cannot live by ideas alone, no matter how eloquently they are stated or argued, but solely by a patient reading and explanation of all of Scripture, line after line, paragraph after paragraph, chapter after chapter, and book after book. Where are such interpreters to be found, and where are their teachers? How long will it be before the people of God rise up in holy horror and say, "Enough, we will no longer tolerate the few scraps that we receive as an excuse for evangelical teaching and preaching."

May God grant to us this kind of hunger, and may He also grant to us this kind of reading and explanation of His Word; for when He does, then the great North American revival cannot be far away.

### FINDING THAT THE JOY OF THE LORD IS OUR STRENGTH (8:9-12)

The entrance of God's Word not only gives light, but it also brings great joy. The first joy that it led to in this revival was a joy that came from being forgiven. On hearing the Word of God read and preached with all of its authenticity and power, the people were deeply convicted of their sin. There was much weeping and lamenting (v. 9). Undoubtedly the portions that must have stirred them most profoundly were those deadly serious texts from Leviticus 26 and Deuteronomy 28, which speak of the alternative prospects of blessing or judgment, depending on the people's response to the Word of God. This produced an ominous sense of impending judgment and of God's deep displeasure with them for the failure to obey Him.

Weeping is not always a sure sign of true repentance, for many weep over being caught or out of sheer embarrassment; here, however, the people wept because they felt the grief their waywardness had caused the Lord. And when the holy standard of God's law was set over against their lives, they cried out in repentance to God. Without this repentance and turning from our sin there can be no revival—ever.

Now when the weeping of the people continued for some time, Ezra, Nehemiah, and the Levites comforted the people by urging them to weep no longer. The word from God was, "This is a day holy to the Lord; do not be grieved, for the joy of the Lord is your strength" (v. 10). Only with great difficulty did they quiet the people, for their grief was deep and sustained.

Authentic declaration of God's Word joined with genuine repentance produces unremitting joy. This kind of joy is not the cheap imitation of the world; it is a holy and satisfying joy that exceeds all boundaries. It is a joy that has its source in the Lord Himself. It is a joy founded on a feeling of being restored and back in communion with Him. It is based on God's goodness and patience (Ex. 34:6-7). This joy is a "stronghold," or a "fortress," which acts as a refuge and a citadel into which the believer can enter no matter what the temperament of the day or the current issues. The Lord Himself serves as our rock and our shelter, both in the time of the storm and in the day-to-day enjoyment of His presence.

Such joy and communion with God easily leads to the sharing of it with others, and thus they sent gifts to those who were without the means to prepare a feast-day meal. Those who had themselves been restored and who had reestablished their own relationships with the Lord could now extend a helping hand in His name to others. In other words, their relational theology and their social involvement was an expression of their propositional theology. The hurts and needs of a battered society can only be met by those who have first had the source and communion of their own joy and fellowship restored.

Once again the Bible deals with the spiritual and temporal needs of individuals and society, but it does insist on a priority in these two tasks. Ernest Baker observed in this connection,

> In all healthy spiritual life these two things go together. George Muller was great at prayer, but equally great in his care for the orphans. C. H. Spurgeon preached to the multitudes; but he also built almshouses and orphanages. General Booth [was] an evangelist of the lapsed masses; but also one who organize[d] relief and rescue works on a large scale. True Christianity is concerned for the people in this world as well as the next. And those who show the deepest concern for the state of the soul are generally those who do most for the people in this present life. The realization of the value of the soul has increased the estimate of the body that enshrines it. We must care for the whole of man.[3]

The joy of the Lord comes, then, because we are forgiven, because we have communion and fellowship with a good Lord, and finally, in verse 12, because we have an understanding of God's Word. So central is this Word for discernment or understanding that it appears six times in this chapter (vv. 2, 3, 7, 8, 9, 12). What greater testimony can be offered for the worthwhileness of faithfully proclaiming God's Word? When God's people understand that Word, there is no containing the holy joy, deep satisfaction, and contentment that overtakes the believing community.

The psalmist wrote, "Great peace have they that love your law, and nothing shall make them stumble" (Ps. 119:165). Thus, emotional and volitional responses must follow, rather than precede, the understanding of the Word of God. It is sad to see how many programs in the church and in society try to reverse this order. But we will never find any real joy or satisfaction in this search until our hearts come to first

3. Ibid., p. 123.

rest in the God who made us, redeemed us, and revealed His Word to us. Only then is there going to be any joy in Mudville or any rejoicing in life or in the Lord.

## UNITING TO PROCLAIM GOD'S FAITHFULNESS (8:13-18)

Invariably, the clear teaching of God's Word has as one of its first by-products the whetting of our appetites for more teaching of that Word. So from the second day until the seventh day of the feast, the people sought out Ezra to hear more (vv. 13, 18). As a result, they learned how to observe the Feast of Tabernacles, or Booths (Lev. 23:33-43). Therefore, on the fifteenth day of the month, each family began cutting down branches from the olive, myrtle, and palm trees to form temporary shelters as they recalled once again the deliverance of God from Egypt. Thus they were united in remembering God's faithfulness in the past. Their unity owed its basis to the enduring strength and joy that came from the Word of God.

Not since the days of Joshua a thousand years before had this festival been held. How complacent the people had grown (v. 17). Now, however, there was true *koinōnia*. A new spirit of sharing, of oneness, and of linking of believers was possible because of the recent work of God's Word in their hearts that had brought repentance. Such unity and fellowship exists in its truest form only in the church or in that group of believers who have united together for the purposes of reading and heeding God's Word. This unity is not the same thing as uniformity, for it still recognizes the diversity of gifts and the uniqueness of personalities. There is no lock-step, cookie-cutter type of regimentation that insists that everyone think or believe precisely as the majority or, worse still, as the leader of the group thinks. This is not a call for conformity or for unanimity on all matters, but it is a call for the softening work of the Spirit of God to unite us around His Word and around Himself and thereby to unite us to one another.

Only two days after they finished celebrating the Feast of Tabernacles, they came to the twenty-fourth day of the seventh month, which is the most holy day, called the Day of Atonement (Lev. 16). This day of fasting they also observed before God (Neh. 9:1-38). They confessed their sins in deep humility before God (9:2), listened to the Word of God again for another three hours (9:3), and entered into another three-hour period of confessing their sins before God (9:3). With an exhortation and an invitation for the congregation to enter into praise and confession, Ezra led the people in one of the longest and most moving prayers in the Bible. So ended the record of one of the longest passages about revival in the Old Testament.

So where do we stand today in this matter of spiritual hunger and biblical appetites? Only when this hunger is excited to the heights seen at this time in Judah will we also in our generation begin to experience the first tastes of revival. Our joy will remain incomplete and without full resonance until we experience the cleansing effects that come from understanding and doing the Word of God. No amount of emotional satisfaction can begin to compare with the totally satisfying joy that comes from knowing that we are wonderfully forgiven, that we now have full fellowship with the living God, and from an understanding of His Word.

Simultaneously with these good gifts will come the desired unity of believers that we have sought for so long. The scandalous divisions that exist within the Body of Christ, not to mention the even more tragic divisions that exist within local churches and Christian institutions, will not be healed until there comes a revival like the one under Nehemiah. We must cry out to God for relief, for much of our efforts in the meantime to still the troubled waters are usually futile.

May our Lord be pleased to visit us with a revival similar to the one He gave under Ezra and Nehemiah. In the meantime, may all who hunger and thirst for righteousness flee to the full teaching of the Word of God. May they cry out in prayer for God's mercy on our communities, crops, nation, and churches. And may they pray so that revival may come soon in the providence and good hand of God.

# Conclusion

The last time America saw such a massive movement of the Spirit of God that would class it with the revivals described in this book was in 1905. For eighty years now we have languished, and the times and conditions become even more acutely desperate. Surely it cannot be a matter for debating: we most assuredly need a nationwide revival in the United States and Canada once again. This is no time for hesitation.

If the need is desperate and the concern of the believing community has begun to mount nationwide with a new desire for a special work of God, what more is needed for revival to come? Because revival truly is the work of God, is it solely a matter of waiting? Can we not also apply to our day the principles learned from the ten great Old Testament revivals and thereby experience just as much of the power and revivifying work of the Spirit of God? Of course we can. That is one of the prime purposes of the Scriptures.

So to the question, "When will revival come?" the prophet Habakkuk has the answer: "In the midst of the years, make [yourself] known [O Lord]; in wrath remember mercy" (Hab. 3:2). In other words, revival will come both in the exact timing of our sovereign Lord and in the moment we have reached a similar extremity and point of desperation as had Judah on the eve of the destruction of Jerusalem. However, when men and women learn to live by faith (Hab. 2:4), then God will once again rain righteousness from heaven on His famished church.[1]

---

1. See the fine chapter and message on Habakkuk 3:2 in Stephen F. Olford, *Heart-Cry for Revival* (Westwood, N. J.: Revell, 1962), pp. 55-64. This volume is more recently published under the title *Lord Open the Heavens* (Wheaton, Ill.: Shaw, 1980).

This only makes the question of how all the more important. No finer answer can be given than our paradigmatic verse from 2 Chronicles 7:14, which laid out the program for each of the revivals that span almost half of the chapters of that great book.

Once we recall that the individuals addressed are "my [God's] people" and that these persons are further defined as all those "who are called by [the Lord's] name," it is clear that our appeal must be to all believers wherever they are and whenever they have lived. It will not be of any help to substitute a program of evangelizing the lost (important as that is on other grounds). Nor will the church be able to excuse herself by protesting that only Israel or Judah was addressed by this verse. The shallowness and wrongheadedness of all of these protestations we have already exposed in the Introduction to this book.

What then must we do in order to be revived—even while we affirm that the work is most decidedly and uniquely the special prerogative of our Lord? We must prepare for that revival by following the four verbs in 2 Chronicles 7:14. The first prerequisite to revival is *humility*. As John R. Mott, that great leader of the student volunteer movement at the turn of the century, so clearly stated it: "Let it be repeated, there are two views of one's life. One is that a man's life is his own, to do with as he [or she] pleases; the other is that it belongs to another and . . . that the other to whom it belongs is Christ Himself."[2] Thus, those who are willing to give their lives to Christ and who in contriteness and lowliness of heart and mind place themselves at the disposal of our great God will be revived in heart and spirit (Isa. 57:15).

The second prerequisite is *prayer*. Sheldon D. Gordon quietly taught us:

> The great people of the earth today are the people who pray. I do not mean those who talk about prayer; nor those who say they believe in prayer; but I mean those people who take time and pray. These are the people today who are doing the most for God; in winning souls; in solving problems; in awakening Churches; in keeping the earth sweet awhile longer.[3]

There can be no substitute for this kind of prayer. The prophet Elijah

2. John R. Mott, *Christian Students and World Problems* (New York: Student Volunteer Movement, 1924), p. 52 as cited by Dan Hayes, *Fireseeds of Spiritual Awakening* (San Bernardino, Calif.: Here's Life, 1983), p. 49.
3. Sheldon D. Gordon, *Quiet Talks on Prayer* (Westwood, N. J.: Revell, 1967), p. 11, as cited by Hayes, *Fireseeds*, p. 73.

can serve as our model, for James 5:17 notes that he, too, was "a man with a nature like ours." But "he prayed earnestly that it might not rain; and it did not rain on the land for three and a half years." James comments, "The prayer of a righteous man worked in [by the Holy Spirit] does accomplish much" (James 5:16). Therefore, we ought to pray for revival.

The third prerequisite is *spiritual hunger*. We must actively seek God's face. Those who hunger and thirst for righteousness will be filled, promised our Lord (Matt. 5:6). Only those who long for a real sense of the presence of God and who are willing to keep pressing their search until they have been touched with a new sense of God's power and cleansing will be among the shakers and movers of this generation for Christ.

The final condition mentioned in 2 Chronicles 7:14 is *confession* and *repentance*. The text boldly calls us to "turn from our wicked ways." Only when we become distressed over the magnitude, the heinousness, and despicable state of our sins personally, institutionally, and nationally will we become likely subjects for revival. Proverbs 28:13 warns, "The person who conceals his [or her] transgressions will not prosper, but the one who confesses and forsakes them will find compassion."

An about-face is most necessary for each believer if we are ever to experience revival. We must change our direction, change our thinking, change our wills, and run to the Savior who alone is able to restore us. This may involve more than the act of the will, mind, and heart. It may go beyond a prayer to our Lord. It may well mean that we should restore what we have stolen, repair the damage we have caused by our slander, or make up for the poor workmanship or services we have rendered. The various means the Lord uses to help us come back to Him will vary, but there may be no variation in the absolute need to return. This command was at the heart of three of the messages to the seven churches in the book of Revelation. Can it be any less for us in our churches today?

May God's people spontaneously and with deep fervency begin meeting His conditions for one more great revival in the United States of America and in Canada before He returns. May you, my reader, be so moved by the Holy Spirit that God may use you as a committee of one to begin now to meet His conditions. My prayer is that in the providence of God, each reader may become an epicenter of one massive spiritual earthquake that will be unequaled by anything we have ever known. Would that not be just like the Lord? Is that not the type of power God has been known for by other generations and in other revivals in the past? Why then should our generation be so rich in so many things but live so far below the poverty level in spiritual quotients?

This depressing state of affairs for both the church and the nations can be halted almost immediately. But everything will depend on how God's people, who are called by His name, act. If they will "humble themselves, and pray, and seek [His] face and turn from their wicked ways," then I am absolutely certain that "[He] will hear from heaven and will forgive [our] sin and will heal [our] land[s]." May it happen quickly.

# Index of Subjects and Persons

# Index of Scripture